Responding to drug and alcohol problems in the community

A manual for primary health care workers with guidelines for trainers

Edited by

Marcus Grant
Programme on Substance Abuse
World Health Organization
Geneva, Switzerland

&

Ray Hodgson
Whitchurch Hospital
Cardiff, Wales

World Health Organization
Geneva 1991

WHO Library Cataloguing in Publication Data

Responding to drug and alcohol problems in the community :
a manual for primary health care workers, with guidelines
for trainers.

1. Substance abuse – prevention and control   2. Alcoholism –
prevention and control   3. Community health aides   4. Community health services.

ISBN 92 4 154427 9   (NLM Classification: WM 270)

© World Health Organization 1991

TYPESET IN INDIA
PRINTED IN ENGLAND

90/8706—Macmillan/Clays—7000

Contents

Preface

In spite of definite improvements in health care in most countries, problems related to drug and alcohol abuse are increasing almost everywhere. No longer can it be argued that these problems must be dealt with only by specialist workers, within a specialized hospital setting. The primary health care service is taking on more and more of the responsibility for dealing with such problems. Furthermore, it is now recognized that a good service involves the integration of medical, psychological and social interventions, since no one profession or group has all the answers. This manual attempts to bring forward the day when primary health care workers are able to coordinate a comprehensive, holistic approach at the community level.

A simple manual for community health workers on drug dependence and alcohol-related problems was produced by the World Health Organization in 1986. That booklet has proved useful in a number of countries and has been used as the basis for the present publication. Many of the themes that were touched upon in the earlier booklet are dealt with more systematically here, and others have been added. The whole approach has also been revised to take account of new thinking on how best to focus primary health care efforts on the prevention and treatment of alcohol and drug problems.

The manual can be used by any member of the primary health care team to improve his or her effectiveness in dealing with drug and alcohol problems. It provides simple guidance on assessing and responding to substance abuse problems at individual, family and community levels. It explains how primary health care services can best be organized and how they can be complemented by other community activities, including those involving the law enforcement sector. It provides information on how to evaluate drug and alcohol programmes. Finally, there are guidelines for trainers of primary health care workers, since it is anticipated that the manual will most often be used in the context of training programmes.

Drug and alcohol problems are among the most challenging for primary health care workers, but they are also most likely to respond to an approach that rests upon the broad principles of primary health care. Most positive changes can be accomplished using the very skills that primary health care workers are accustomed to applying in the rest of their work. The purpose of this manual is to show how these skills can be used most effectively in preventing and treating drug and alcohol problems. In the end, however, the success of this manual will depend upon the willingness of primary health care workers to learn from each other and from their patients.

A number of authors contributed the initial drafts of different chapters of this book. These were: Dr W. Acuda (Zimbabwe), Dr M. Argondona (Bolivia), Dr R. Denniston (United States of America), Dr N. Kodogoda (Sri Lanka), Dr J. Makanjuola (Nigeria), Dr D. Mohan (India) and Dr V. Navaratnam (Malaysia). Their drafts were the subject of an extensive process of comment, consultation and pilot-testing, after which the chapters were redrafted by the editors, to form an integrated text. Among those who assisted in the review process were Dr Charas Suwanwela, Dr R. Gonzales, Dr M. Gossop, Dr D. Hilton, Dr V. Hudolin, and Mrs S. Kapoor. The finalization of the text was facilitated by Mrs E. Duane, Mrs D. Hodgson and Ms L. Honda. In addition to expressing gratitude to all those individuals, the editors thank the United Nations Fund for Drug Abuse Control, which provided the financial support that made the preparation and publication of this book possible.

1. Assessment of drug and alcohol abuse in the individual and the family

Primary health care (PHC) workers in countries around the world differ markedly in their levels of training and skill. The common factor about them is that they are all very busy people, able to devote only a few minutes or so to each patient. They are also expected to handle all the health and social problems that arise in their area. These problems will almost certainly include substance abuse, which seems to be on the increase in many parts of the world. PHC workers are coming into contact with these problems with increasing frequency and are expected to deal with them.

The purpose of this chapter is therefore:

- to increase the awareness of PHC workers to the possible existence of substance abuse among members of their community;
- to help them explore (or rule out) the possibility of substance abuse in their patients;
- to provide PHC workers with the skills to recognize substance use disorders by thorough assessment of patients and their families, and to formulate a plan of action.

The importance of this assessment cannot be overemphasized. The recognition of substance abuse is the first and most important step in the management and prevention of these problems. The assessment process, however, is not always straightforward. While the prototype of the "alcoholic" or the "drug addict" ("junkie") may not be difficult to recognize, such patients are relatively few, and the average PHC worker is not likely to come across them frequently. The majority of drug-dependent persons, particularly those in the early stages, can be very difficult to recognize. The psychological, social, and physical manifestations vary widely, depending on the particular substance or substances used, the amounts used or frequency of use, and other factors, such as the age and physical health of the user. The early stages of substance abuse

1

may mimic the symptoms of many psychiatric and physical illnesses, such as anxiety, depression, paranoia, and vague physical complaints.

This chapter will guide the PHC worker through these specific problems and provide a framework for the assessment interview. The overall objective is to facilitate effective treatment and rehabilitation of the patient once the problem has been recognized.

This manual will help to:

- increase awareness of drug and alcohol problems,
- encourage the PHC worker to explore drug and alcohol problems,
- develop appropriate skills to assess these problems and formulate an action plan.

Importance of the primary care setting

The use and abuse of psychoactive substances have increased considerably in many parts of the world in recent years, and drug and alcohol abuse now constitutes a very serious public health and socioeconomic problem in many countries. In developing countries, the situation is even more acute, because, despite the magnitude of the problem, the resources necessary to combat it remain very scarce.

The harmful consequences of substance abuse are numerous. They can be physical (hepatitis), psychological (depression and suicide), or social (crime). They can affect the individual, the family, and the community. Substance abuse disorders, therefore, cannot be dealt with adequately by any single health profession or group. Physicians, general practitioners, nurses, and other primary health care workers are increasingly coming into contact with patients who have these problems, in the various settings where they work. Furthermore, chemically dependent persons suffer more ill health than others, and consequently make more use of primary health care facilities. This makes the primary health care setting an ideal place for the identification and management of these problems.

In addition, the primary health care setting avoids the problem of stigma, because the primary health care workers can usually manage drug and alcohol problems as part of general health care. There is also evidence that many health problems, including substance abuse disorders, are seen at the PHC facility at an early stage when successful treatment may still be easy to achieve, thus saving on the costs involved in treatment at a later stage, which can require hospitalization. In many countries, a member of the family usually accompanies the patient to the PHC clinic. This provides an opportunity for family contact, which is often crucial in the assessment and management of substance abuse.

Why the primary care setting?

- Drug and alcohol problems are too widespread to be dealt with by a small specialized service.
- Drug and alcohol abusers frequently visit the primary health care facility.
- The primary care setting avoids the stigma associated with a drug-dependence, alcohol-dependence, or mental illness service.
- Early identification and treatment are more likely.
- The setting facilitates contact with the family and the community.

The current trend to decentralize the health care services as much as possible to the community provides the opportunity for primary health care workers to play a leading role in the management of these problems.

Aims of the assessment

The assessment of substance use disorders begins with the first contact between the primary health care worker and the individual (the patient), and his or her family. The patient may have been referred to the health worker by a parent, friend, relative, general practitioner, teacher, law enforcement officer, or other social agency. On the other hand, first contact with the patient may take place in a hospital setting, such as the emergency room or ward, where the patient might have presented with physical illness (drug-related or non-drug-related) or social problems.

The main aims of an assessment are:

- To obtain as much accurate information as possible about the individual's drug use and any associated problems.
- To try to identify the factors associated with drug abuse in the individual—these may be physical illnesses, or social or psychological problems.
- To assist the PHC worker in identifying the strengths and weaknesses of the individual and his or her family, as well as their ability to cope with, and assist in the management of, the problem.

3

Information about the individual and the family will help the PHC worker to determine the most appropriate approach to treatment, and to mobilize support from the family and the community. It is important for the PHC worker to know how the individual and his or her family are functioning now, and how they have been functioning in the recent past.

The PHC worker should bear in mind that every drug abuser is different, and that an individual programme plan must be formulated for each one.

The first interview

An assessment interview usually takes place during the first meeting, and has a very significant influence on the patient's expectations. Whenever possible, the interview should take place in private, and confidentiality must be guaranteed. Although in many cases the patient should be seen first, a joint interview with the patient's spouse, or other relatives, is often preferred by the patient and the family.

The first interview has a significant influence on the patient's expectations.

Apart from its value in assessing the patient, the interview itself can be therapeutic. It gives the patient, or the family, the opportunity to air their feelings, or to describe the problem, and helps the patient to identify and define the problem more clearly.

From the beginning of the interview, the primary health care worker must remember that while, in some cases, the patient may have come for treatment voluntarily, in others the interview may have been suggested by, for example, parents (or guardians and other relatives), teachers, or a juvenile court. Consultation may also have been precipitated by a crisis, such as a suicide attempt, an accident, the discovery of a drug, or public drunkenness in school, at home, or at work. The primary health care worker should therefore be alert to the possibility that the patient may be uncooperative or even overtly hostile and defensive.

Interviewing technique

The PHC worker should treat patients with respect, and should avoid confrontation or an authoritarian approach. It is important to acknowledge the patient's feelings, and at certain stages even to "agree to disagree" with the patient if confrontation seems imminent, but still to proceed with the assessment. At all times, the patient must feel that his or her problems are the PHC worker's primary concern. The PHC worker should avoid plunging directly into the topic of substance abuse.

If the patient is angry, suspicious or hostile, seems to feel that he or she has already been "reported" or "judged", and chooses not to talk or denies any problem, the PHC worker should provide reassurance along the following lines:

"Every story has two sides. So far we have heard one side of it from . . . Now, I would very much like to hear your version."

or

"Your parents (or teachers) are concerned about you. How do you feel about their concern?"

or

"You seem quite upset about coming here; I understand why you are feeling like this."

These statements can relieve anxiety, reduce suspicion, and may encourage cooperation.

As much as possible, the patient should be encouraged to tell his or her own story. If, for example, a teenager uses a street language unknown to the PHC worker he or she should politely ask the patient to elaborate. If

5

patients try to divert discussions, and concentrate on the problems of relatives or friends, the PHC worker should listen for a while, but then interrupt: *"I understand your being concerned about . . . , and we will talk more about that later, but right now tell me about. . . ."*

When the sensitive issue of drug use comes up, the PHC worker should be very careful. It is less threatening to begin by discussing the use of socially acceptable drugs such as tobacco or alcohol, and proceed to the use of medically prescribed drugs, such as benzodiazepines, before moving on to unsanctioned drugs, such as marijuana, cocaine, etc. Many patients minimize or deny the extent of their drug involvement, or distort information. This can often be overcome by asking questions in a non-threatening style. Detailed questioning about quantities consumed should be avoided at the beginning of the interview. Instead patients should be encouraged to talk about their feelings, through questions such as:

"Do you occasionally use drugs or drink heavily after a disappointment or a quarrel, or when your boss gives you a hard time?"

"Are there certain occasions when you feel uncomfortable if alcohol or drugs are not available?"

"Do you sometimes feel a little guilty about your drug use or drinking?"

"Do you often regret things that you have done or said while drinking or using drugs?"

"Have you often failed to keep promises that you have made to yourself about cutting down your drug or alcohol use?"

Ask the patient for specific examples; the answers will make it easier to build up a clear picture of the problem.

When the patient is ready and willing, the PHC worker should ask the patient about the circumstances in which he or she first used drugs. The health worker can then gradually approach the question of current use—type of drugs used, quantity, frequency, and duration of use.

Use and abuse of drugs should be discussed thoroughly, and any resulting problems and complications should be highlighted. The PHC worker should at this stage be able to relate drug abuse to the patient's current and past problems.

High-risk groups and indirect indicators of drug problems

Not all people with a drug abuse problem will come to the PHC facility for that specific reason. Many will present indirectly with other problems of a medical or social nature. The PHC worker must be on the look-out for these indirect presentations, as well as for individuals from certain groups known to be at risk of drug problems. Should the PHC worker come across such patients, it is important to probe further into their drug history. The presence of any of the following could indicate a potential drug-related problem:

- medical conditions known to be associated with drug or alcohol abuse, e.g., pancreatitis, liver disease, gastritis, morning nausea and vomiting, recurrent diarrhoea;
- drug overdose (suicide attempt or accidental poisoning);
- certain psychiatric symptoms (anxiety, depression, phobias, panic attacks, paranoia, impotence, hallucinations, confusion, loss of memory, violence, abnormal behaviour, or "psychosis");
- the above conditions in a patient admitted as an emergency case, especially associated with injuries, or loss of consciousness;
- legal problems related to drinking (e.g., drink-driving offences);
- epileptic fits occurring for the first time after adolescence;
- a history of recent drastic changes in level of functioning at work or at home, or a sudden change in "personality";
- excessive interest in certain drugs, or presentation of false prescriptions;
- a history of frequent absenteeism from work.

In addition, the PHC worker should ask routinely about general health problems, in particular the following:

- low energy
- chest congestion
- sleep problems
- headaches
- trembling hands
- sinus congestion
- sore throat
- runny nose
- heart flutters
- nausea
- chills
- excessive weight loss
- loss of sex drive.

Additional information

Whether the patient is fully cooperative during the interview or not, the PHC worker should try to obtain additional information from independent sources, not only to corroborate information from the patient, but also to provide a different viewpoint. A relative is often an excellent source of information and will sometimes provide a clear description of the extent of the problem. When the subject of drugs is brought up, the relative might be asked the following questions:

- Do you worry about his/her drinking or drug use?
- Have you ever been embarrassed by it?

- Does he/she often promise to stop using drugs or alcohol, without success?
- Have you ever lied to an employer, relatives, or friends in order to hide his/her drinking or drug use?
- Are children afraid of the patient while he/she is using drugs or drinking?

In order to get a detailed and vivid picture of the social effects of drug or alcohol use, ask the relative to provide specific examples.

Interviewing the family

The family can be gravely damaged, or even destroyed, by excessive use of, or dependence on, psychoactive substances by any one of its members. The damage can result from the immediate effects of substance abuse, such as violence resulting from intoxication, or the long-term effects, such as family discord and breakdown resulting from chronic dependence. If any one member of the family becomes dependent on a psychoactive substance, the whole family will be affected in one way or another. In many cases, the family will have undergone a considerable amount of stress long before the problem becomes obvious to outsiders. Also, it is often a member of the family — a parent or spouse — who makes the initial contact with the PHC worker. Usually during the first assessment interview, the family is in a crisis that requires immediate intervention, and the PHC worker should be aware of this fact.

To a large extent, the general principles of assessment of the family are not very different from those of assessment of the patient. In certain circumstances, the initial assessment will have taken place in the presence of the family member or a relative. More frequently, the family member or the spouse can be interviewed immediately after the patient. In either case, the first interview with the family should be as therapeutic as possible.

The PHC worker should encourage the family members to tell their own story, and should guide them in recounting specific incidents that have led to the referral. Family members should be encouraged to describe and discuss the impact of drug abuse on the victim and on themselves. At the same time, the PHC worker should attempt to assess the degree of stability or instability in the family, and to build up a picture of the family's ability to cope.

The PHC worker should try to find out whether other members of the family use psychoactive substances. Just as the patient can become uncooperative, and deny the existence of a problem, a similar situation may be encountered during a family assessment, and a "conspiracy of

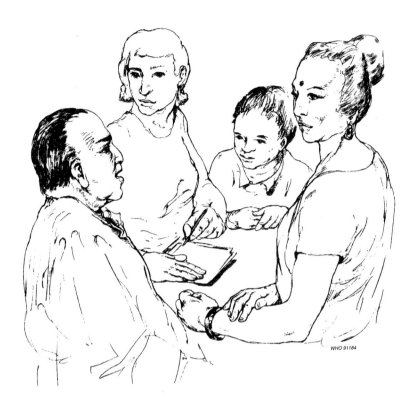

The PHC worker should encourage family members to tell their own story.

silence" can exist. The PHC worker has to be tactful in dealing with this situation.

Alcohol problems in the family, especially among parents, may go undetected for years, while individual members of the family continue to experience stress. Although some families may present directly and voluntarily with the problem, in many cases the PHC worker will have to look for indirect indicators of drug or alcohol abuse in the family, often referred to as "secondary signs and symptoms" of alcohol problems.

These indicators include:

- repeated violence to the spouse or children;
- marital discord or separation;
- financial problems;
- child neglect;
- academic deterioration of children at school;

9

- delinquent behaviour in children, including drug abuse and truancy;
- history of drug or alcohol abuse in relatives.

The presence of any of these indicators should prompt the PHC worker to probe more deeply into the family's use of alcohol and drugs, if such information has not been volunteered.

Assessment as a basis for action

The PHC worker should have in mind a broad plan to guide the assessment process. The plan should be derived from the treatment strategy, since good assessment provides the basis for action. The following is one commonly used strategy for treatment, involving five points:

- improving social relationships and supports;
- developing confidence in ability to change;
- identifying reasons to change;
- developing alternative activities;
- learning to prevent relapse.

Helping people to change is covered in Chapter 5, but the PHC worker should be thinking about formulating an action plan even during the first interview. The assessment should be designed to collect useful information linked to the five components of treatment listed above.

One way of remembering these five points

Remember the word **SCRAP** which stands for:

S = social relationships
C = confidence in ability to change
R = reasons to change
A = alternative activities
P = preventing relapse

The questions listed below, under five headings, will help the PHC worker to collect relevant information and formulate an action plan in each of these areas.

Social relationships

Ask questions such as the following:

"If you are feeling bored or depressed, do you have a friend, or friends, that you can talk to?"

"Is there a family member who is able to give you help and support?"

"If you wanted to go for a long walk, play sport, see a film, etc., is there a friend, or friends, that you could ask to go with you?"

"Are there any clubs that you could join?"

"Do you know anybody who would be willing to help you for the next six months?" (e.g., member of Alcoholics Anonymous, relative, priest, or friend).

Confidence in ability to change

Here, the aim is to explore the feelings of helplessness that a client might be experiencing. Ask the following:

"Have you tried to cut down, or stop, your drug or alcohol use? How successful were you?"

"In the future, if you were able to stop taking drugs or alcohol for two weeks, and then experienced a strong desire to start again, how confident are you that you could resist?"

Reasons to change

When an action plan is devised, the first essential is to obtain the client's commitment to change. A good assessment should therefore explore the client's perception of the reasons why changes need to be made. Questions such as the following might be appropriate.

"If you were to stop, or reduce, your drug/alcohol use:

- *Do you think that you would sleep better?*
- *Would your marriage improve?*
- *Would you live longer?*
- *Would you save a lot of money?*
- *Would your relationships improve?*
- *Do you think that you would achieve more in your life?*
- *Would you be better at your job?"*

The PHC worker should attempt to assess the importance of these expected consequences. For example, a client might say, "Yes, my marriage would improve, but I don't care."

Alternative activities

If a drug user, or heavy drinker, is going to change dramatically, then an alternative life-style will have to be developed. This involves a little planning, and questioning along the following lines might help to pinpoint possible activities:

"What types of things have you enjoyed learning in the past?" (e.g., sports, chess, languages).

"What types of trips have you enjoyed in the past?" (e.g., to the sea, to the mountains, to the country).

"What types of things do you think you could enjoy if you had no worries about failing?" (e.g., painting, acting, playing a musical instrument).

"What have you enjoyed doing alone?" (e.g., long walks, playing a musical instrument, sewing).

"What have you enjoyed doing with others?" (e.g., talking, having a meal with a friend, playing table-tennis).

"What have you enjoyed doing that costs no money?" (e.g., playing with a dog, going to the library, reading).

"What have you enjoyed doing that costs very little?" (e.g., going to a museum, taking a short bus ride).

"What activities have you enjoyed at different times?" (e.g., in the morning, on Sunday, in the spring, in autumn).

Preventing relapse

The desire to use drugs or alcohol heavily goes up and down depending on mood, the availability of drugs, and the social setting. The PHC worker should explain this and attempt to identify the main high-risk situations or cues. The following list will help:

● Parties	● Criticism	● Family	● Particular
● Feeling lonely	● Moods	● After work	people
● Boredom	● Places	● Arguments	● Sleeplessness
● When others are using drugs	● Feeling of failure	● Tension	● Weekends

In addition, the following questions will help to pinpoint relapse situations, thoughts, and mood.

"Would you be able to resist using drugs or drinking heavily if:

- *something good happened and you felt like celebrating?*
- *you suddenly remembered how good you can feel after taking drugs or alcohol?*

- *other people treated you unfairly?*
- *you were having problems with people at work?*
- *someone criticized you?*
- *you were having arguments at home?"*

The information collected on social relationships, confidence in ability to change, reasons to change, alternative activities, and high-risk situations will be very helpful when an individual treatment programme is being devised.

Summary

The PHC worker might feel that the assessment outlined above is much too lengthy to be carried out during a first contact of less than half-an-hour. If so, the following points should be remembered. First it is surprising how much can be covered in half-an-hour when the interviewer is skilled. Secondly, some of the questions might be irrelevant for a particular client. Finally, remember that assessment and treatment or counselling can go on together. If the PHC worker sees a client on four or five occasions, then a part of each session should be devoted to continued assessment.

In summary, an assessment involves the following steps:

- allow at least 30 minutes for each client with a drug or alcohol problem (one hour if possible);
- establish trust;
- assure the client of confidentiality;
- ask about general health problems;
- encourage clients to describe recent experiences;
- interview family, assess family;
- remember SCRAP.

---

2. Assessment of drug and alcohol abuse at the community level

In many communities, the main causes of premature death are cardio-vascular diseases, cancers, accidents, and suicides, all of which may be related to drug and alcohol abuse. It follows that primary health care workers who are attempting to promote healthy life-styles will need to develop ways of preventing the excessive and inappropriate use of a wide range of drugs, including alcohol and tobacco.

This chapter provides information that will enable a primary health worker to acquire the basic skills needed to:

- recognize and assess the health and social problems that are related to the use of psychoactive substances;
- establish the extent and nature of such problems, the attitudes within the community towards them, and any existing and potential resources that could be utilized in developing a community action programme;
- establish priorities in initiating interventions; and
- identify ways of monitoring change.

When planning an assessment of drug and alcohol abuse in a community, it will help if the following simple view is kept in mind. An assessment should attempt to identify the factors that *increase the risk* and those that *reduce the risk* of drug abuse, as well as the nature and extent of the abuse.

Risk is increased if:

- Friends abuse drugs.
- Drugs are cheap and easily available.
- Very pleasant effects are expected.

Risk is reduced if:

- Police are vigilant.
- Church and school are concerned.
- Harmful effects are acknowledged.

A thorough assessment is essential, even if time and resources are very limited. Without such an assessment, it might be difficult to persuade key people to take action, and a great deal of effort could be directed towards the wrong targets.

Why assessment is so important

- An assessment provides information about the extent of the problem, as well as about the changes that a community needs to make (e.g., what percentage of crimes and accidents is associated with drug or alcohol use).
- Opinion leaders and managers of services and other agencies (e.g., police and social workers) can be influenced by such information.
- Good information can suggest useful approaches to influencing the community (e.g., an accident prevention campaign).
- Changes in a community's use of drugs and alcohol can be monitored.

Commonly abused substances

Some of the substances that are commonly abused are described in detail in Annex 1, while Table 1 provides a summary of the main types.

Table 1. Types of abused substances

Type of substance	Examples	Effect
Depressants	Alcohol, barbiturates, sedatives, sleeping tablets	Drowsiness, pleasant relaxation, disinhibition
Opiates	Morphine, methadone	Relief of pain, pleasant, detached, dreamy euphoria
Stimulants	Cocaine, amfetamines	Exhilaration, reduced fatigue and hunger
Hallucinogenics	LSD, mescaline, peyote	Other-worldliness, perceptual distortions
Cannabis	Marijuana, ganja, bhang	Relaxation and hallucinogenic effects
Nicotine	Tobacco	Sedation and stimulation
Volatile inhalants	Glues, lacquers, paint thinners	Drowsiness, relaxation, perceptual disturbances

15

Routes of drug administration

There are several different ways in which drugs may be taken into the body; they may be swallowed (eaten or drunk), chewed and absorbed through the lining of the mouth, sniffed and absorbed through the lining of the nose, inhaled through the lungs, or injected—either beneath the skin, into the muscles, or into a vein. Some drugs can be taken in several different ways. Tobacco may be chewed, sniffed as snuff, or smoked, while cocaine may be chewed (as coca leaves), sniffed, smoked, or injected.

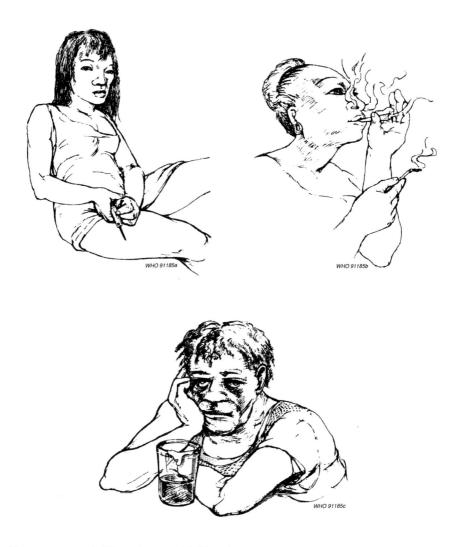

There are several different ways of taking drugs.

These different methods of introducing drugs into the body have important implications for drug effects, risk of dependence, and risks to health. Traditional cultures often accept, or approve of, the use of a swallowed or chewed drug (opium eating, for example, or cannabis when drunk or eaten, or cocaine when chewed), but mildly disapprove of the smoking of a drug (opium or cannabis smoking), and absolutely disapprove of the injection of drugs (e.g., heroin).

This type of instinctive cultural appraisal seems generally to be based on a fairly accurate assessment of relative risks. A substance that is eaten will produce effects that are far less rapid in onset and less intense than those produced by the same drug when injected, with inhalation usually giving an intermediate effect. Opium when eaten gives nothing like the "buzz" or "rush" of a heroin injection, but a much steadier level of intoxication. Methods of administration that have been used traditionally will therefore carry less risk of rapid dependence. Opium-eating, for instance, certainly implies some risk of dependence, but it may be possible to eat opium over a fairly prolonged period without becoming dependent; smoking of opium is likely to cause more serious social incapacity, and more rapid and less tractable dependence; intravenous injection of heroin is usually not compatible with normal social functioning, and carries risks of a fatal overdose and of speedy and major dependence.

Methods of assessment

Four main approaches can be used to obtain evidence and information about drug and alcohol problems. One approach is simply to collate existing information, which might be available at a health centre or enforcement agency, for example. Another method is to interview knowledgeable key informants. The key informants could be community leaders, nurses, doctors, or enforcement officials who are in contact with individuals or groups involved in drug or alcohol abuse. An important approach that complements both of these methods is a procedure known as participant observation, in which the PHC worker, or volunteer, observes the occurrence of drug or alcohol abuse or substance-related problems (see page 23 for details). Another method is to organize a general population survey of the community to identify (a) how many respondents use drugs or abuse alcohol, and (b) whether certain drug- or alcohol-related problems exist. Perceptions about the use of drugs and alcohol and attitudes towards abuse can also be ascertained.

Methods of assessment

Existing information
Key informants
Participant observation
Community survey

With all of these approaches, it is essential to realize the limitations of the methods. For example, hospital information relates to people coming for treatment, and will not indicate the extent and pattern of abuse in general. Similarly, interviewing key informants has its limitations; there might be a tendency to hide embarrassing information or, on the other hand, to exaggerate the situation. Even community surveys can produce distorted results, since there is likely to be underreporting by those who have serious problems related to substance abuse.

In order to gain a balanced perspective, it is essential that more than one approach is used; however, an overriding factor will be the availability of appropriate resources.

Collating existing information

Useful information probably exists in most communities. For example, information on the consumption of legal drugs, such as analgesics, can be obtained from health centres or hospitals, as well as from local pharmacies. Information on the numbers of persons arrested for possession of illegal drugs can be obtained from the local enforcement agency. The very first task, therefore, is to think about the types of information that need to be collated.

What information is needed?

A useful first step in exploring the information requirements of a community is to contact a few knowledgeable community leaders and obtain informal impressions of existing problems and issues. The next step is to use these problems and issues to form specific questions. For example, there might be some concern that there is a high truancy rate among children at secondary schools associated with cannabis abuse.

This concern could be broken down into a series of questions such as the following:

- Is there a problem of truancy among schoolchildren?
- Is the problem of truancy limited only to children at secondary schools and, if so, is it associated with any particular age group or school level?

- Are there any particular characteristics of those schoolchildren who play truant (e.g., do they come from unhappy homes)?
- How many of these truant children abuse cannabis, and how many schoolchildren abuse cannabis but do not manifest a truancy problem?
- For how long did these schoolchildren abuse cannabis before they showed truancy behaviour?

When collecting information, it is desirable to ensure that general, as well as drug- or alcohol-specific, information is collected. For example, if road traffic accidents appear to be a serious problem related to substance abuse in a given community, it is essential to obtain information on the total number of road traffic accidents occurring over a given period (general information). The number of road traffic accidents that involved persons who were abusing drugs or alcohol (substance-specific information) is also required. With this information, it is possible to assess (a) whether there is a significant problem due to road traffic accidents, and (b) the extent to which the accidents are linked to abuse of drugs or alcohol.

The following examples indicate the types of information that could be collated from a variety of sources:

- The availability of psychoactive substances in the community, and the ease with which they can be obtained.
- The extent to which abuse of the various psychoactive substances occurs.
- The types of people who are involved in abuse.
- The types of social and health problems that are related to the abuse of psychoactive substances.
- Key people with an interest in the prevention of drug and alcohol abuse.
- Existing programmes or activities that are available to the abusers. What do they offer?
- Available or potential resources that are appropriate and could be used in a programme of action.
- The legal position regarding the substances being abused, and that of those who abuse them.
- The control measures, if any, that exist, and the extent to which they are applied.

Potential sources of information

Information on psychoactive substance abuse may be available from a number of sources, including health clinics (centres), social service agencies, government statistics offices, enforcement agencies, pharmacies, and retail outlets. Most of these agencies keep records of some sort.

Information on the sale of alcohol can be obtained from the distributors or the licensing authority, and possibly from the taxation branch of the government. Similarly, information on the sale of drugs can often be obtained from hospital and private pharmacies or even doctors. Information about the availability of illicit drugs might be obtainable from the police, or an equivalent agency.

Hospitals and doctors will have information on the types of persons who seek assistance because of drug- or alcohol-related problems. Similarly, police sources will have information on persons who have been involved in drug- or alcohol-related accidents or crime. The courts will have information on people who have been charged with offences related to use of drugs or alcohol. Social agencies, such as "crisis" centres, religious and voluntary service groups (e.g., Red Cross) may also have relevant information. In addition, they may be aware of assistance or treatment programmes or facilities that are available locally.

Heads of schools and colleges will have information on young people who are experiencing difficulties due to substance abuse. They might also be aware of any researchers who have examined problems of substance abuse, or of people who might be interested in being associated with a community assessment programme.

Community administration authorities, e.g., the village or town council, will probably have information on the funds spent on social programmes, damage to property caused by persons involved in substance abuse, as well as available facilities and resources that might be of use in programme development.

Obtaining the information

Having identified the possible sources of information, access has to be gained. The first step is to make contact with a key authority in the agency and inform him or her of the objectives of the assessment exercise, the importance of it, and how the information gathered by the agency could contribute to the study. Ensure that, if required, confidentiality is respected and appropriate acknowledgement is made. This last aspect is particularly important if the official has to devote time and other resources to retrieving the needed information. Develop a good working relationship with the agency staff.

Having gained access to the information, it is important to assess its quality. There may be a large amount of information, but many of the records may be incomplete. To facilitate the data collection process, it is useful to list what kinds of information are available, and then design a

standard form. This will ensure that information is collected systematically, and also that the amount of missing data can be assessed.

In gathering the information, it is important that any particular
characteristics of the source be identified (e.g., overdose cases). Whenever
possible, an attempt should be made to compare the data with similar
data from a matched group, for example, compare drug abusers in prison
with non-drug-abusers imprisoned for similar crimes.

Key informant approach

Basically, this approach entails interviewing a selected group of individuals who have specialized knowledge of, or involvement with, drug and
alcohol abuse problems. These individuals are asked to talk about their
knowledge and perceptions of the problem.

The key informants could be the community chief, a medical or social
worker in the community, a local police officer, a headman, a community
leader, or a politician. This approach can be used to gather both general
and specific information on the subject. For example, it is appropriate to
inquire generally about the problems of young people, as well as the extent
of cannabis use by young people.

This approach can be used to generate information relatively easily
and at minimal cost, but it should be remembered that the method relies
entirely on the reports of people who themselves could be described as
"observers". Their reports will be distorted by incomplete knowledge,
personal bias, and inaccurate estimations. Hence, if this approach is
adopted, it is important that (a) informants are selected with extreme care
to ensure that their views fairly reflect the real situation, and (b) the
information obtained is checked with other informants, or by other
assessment methods. If one informant states that 50% of all crimes in the
community are committed by heroin abusers, this should be validated by
data from the enforcement agency or with other key persons, including
enforcement officials.

The key informant approach, if properly used, has several advantages.
It can generate general and specific information on the subject at
relatively low cost. Also, it produces information on acceptable cultural
practices, as well as a description of problems.

Objectives and information needs

The main objective may be to obtain information about drug or alcohol
abuse or resultant problems in the community. Alternatively, the interviews can be focused more on a particular substance, a particular

21

subpopulation, or even a programme. It is extremely important that the objectives are clearly defined prior to the commencement of the study.

The following are some examples of topics that could be explored with key informants:

- How is drug or alcohol abuse perceived in the community? Is it thought to be a problem or not? Who are the people involved? What types of substance are abused? What are the perceived problems? Do these problems affect only certain individuals or the community as a whole?
- Approximately how many people known to the informant have problems related to drug or alcohol abuse? How many of these individuals have specific problems related to abuse, for example, infections, cirrhosis of the liver, poor nutritional status, abnormal behaviour, or difficulties in personal relationships? Are they mainly men or women— of what age groups and of what occupational, educational and marital status?
- What quantitative information is available on the amount and frequency of substance abuse (if possible, by substance type); at what age are substances first used, how are they consumed, what is the frequency of the different problems manifested by abusers.
- How does the informant and/or the community view substance abuse? Is the use of certain substances acceptable, while use of others is completely forbidden? (For example, in some cultures alcohol is prohibited but the use of opium is tolerated.)
- What kind of facilities are available for treatment of substance abusers? What kind of services are available in these facilities? How do they function and how are they funded? How does one gain access to these resources, and who does one approach?

Having outlined the kind of information required, the next step is to draft a series of questions to elicit it. Keep the questions simple. Break down complex questions into a series of simple questions. Try to make the questions follow a systematic sequence; for example:

- Are you aware of substance abuse problems in your community?
- Do you know anyone who is involved?
- What are the substances being abused?
- How many people do you think are involved?
- Are these people having any problems?
- Are any of these problems caused by substance abuse?

Design a strategy for selecting specific people for interview. If possible, they should represent diverse social, economic, educational, and occupational backgrounds. Obviously, it would be advantageous to select people who are associated with agencies or voluntary organizations that might have contact with substance abusers, for example, police officers, doctors, social workers, community leaders, teachers, or religious leaders.

If hired staff or helpers are used to carry out the interviews, it is essential to give clear instructions on how to make appointments, complete the questionnaire, and validate the responses. The interviewer should also be told the objectives and purpose of the interview, and given some training in how to conduct it, e.g., to elicit responses without leading the individual.

In summary, the key informant approach has several advantages. It can be carried out quickly and is capable of generating information on a wide range of general and specific topics. However, it is essential that the data gathered are validated by cross-checking with others or by other methods. It is an approach that should be used in conjunction with other techniques.

Participant observation

This technique calls for an individual or group of individuals to locate themselves within a community or group, and record their observations. A few examples of the types of information that can be obtained through participant observation are given below.

- An observer at a party could estimate how many people drink and drive.
- A nurse in an accident and emergency department of a hospital could describe the way in which doctors and nurses assess drug and alcohol use. What advice is given to drug and alcohol abusers?
- An observer in a bar could record the rate at which alcohol is consumed at adjoining tables.
- A student could observe the drinking habits of fellow students.
- An industrial worker could provide information on the lunch-time consumption of alcohol or cannabis.

The main advantage of participant observation is that behaviour is observed directly; there is no need to rely on impressions or rumours.

The observation should be unobtrusive and the observer must be an accepted member of the group. The data gathered relate to patterns of behaviour. The exercise is not an attempt to identify people at risk, and care must be taken to ensure that individuals are not identified in any written report.

The observer should make notes as frequently as possible and should attempt to record exactly what happens. It may be necessary to leave the scene, when appropriate, in order to record the observations.

A full record of a participant observation session involving drug use might include the following information:

- A description of the setting and the people involved (e.g., workplace, bar).
- How many people are using alcohol or a specific drug? How many are not?
- Information on price and availability of the drug.
- How are the substances consumed (e.g., smoked, chewed, inhaled)?
- Does drug use lead to any problems (e.g., accidents, violence)?
- Is there a leader or role model? Are some drug users encouraged to use more than they planned to?

This approach has a number of limitations, since it involves specific social settings, which might be atypical. Nevertheless, the observer is a part of the action and is not building up a picture through rumours or second-hand reporting. The approach provides evidence to complement the information gathered using other methods.

Community and special population surveys

In this approach, information is collected systematically from representatives of a given community. The approach is more complex than the other three and also much more structured. The results are therefore more easily quantifiable. A "community" can be defined as a fixed population or grouping, e.g., a village, town, or canton. A "special population" can refer to a group of people who have common traits or behavioural patterns, for example, prisoners, the mentally ill, school drop-outs, the unemployed, or other similar groups.

The survey approach provides a description of, and to some extent quantitative information about, the population being studied, as well as about substance abuse and related problems at the time of the survey. It is a very useful approach, because the information generated can serve as a baseline for future studies. It is then possible to measure changes in the extent of abuse, attitudes to the abuse, and associated problems.

It must be reiterated that this approach requires careful planning and implementation, and is likely to be expensive. It is, therefore, advisable to obtain the assistance of universities, colleges, research centres, or professional groups with some experience of the survey approach.

The following are examples of important factors that should be taken into account when a survey is being planned:

- An attempt should be made to survey a *representative sample* of the population being studied. For example, in a community consisting of

Collect information from representatives of the community.

100 houses, the occupants of every fifth house could be included in the survey. There are also more complicated methods of ensuring that a sample is truly representative.

● There are risks involved in *extrapolating results* from one sample to another. For example, another similar-sized community might be different in many ways (e.g., age distribution and social class, as well as drug use).

● Some questions will require a simple *quantifiable response*, but there should also be questions that allow a more qualitative and *unstructured* response (e.g., "describe in your own words what help should be provided for young people who are abusing drugs").

● In drafting questions, it is essential to design them specifically to fit the objectives of the study and the target population. It is equally important that they are clear and specific. The question, "How often do you use drugs?" will provide answers that are difficult to interpret. It is better to ask a series of questions, such as the following: "Which of these drugs have you used during the last month: cannabis, alcohol, cigarettes, heroin, cocaine?" "How many times during the last month have you used (i) cannabis (ii) alcohol?"

25

- Prior to the collection of data, it is important to develop some *standardized procedures*. This will minimize errors in recording and reporting, and ensure comparability of data. The procedures should clearly state how to conduct the interview, including how to obtain informed consent. If the interviewer is expected to record or code the responses, then instructions must be given on how to do this.
- In spite of detailed attention to the design and testing of the question-naire, there are bound to be unexpected problems, especially mistakes and inadequate record-keeping. It is, therefore, useful to *check randomly* some of the returned questionnaires, and if necessary carry out repeat interviews on a few people to ensure reliability of recording.
- Another common problem occurs when other people are present during the interview. Under these circumstances the respondent might be evasive. Whenever possible, the interview should be conducted in private; if this is not possible, the circumstances should be indicated.

In summary, surveys can generate a wealth of valuable information. They can be used to obtain general and specific information, including information relating to attitudes, awareness of resources, and other associated matters. Because of the complexities involved, a survey might be carried out in conjunction with an experienced agency. Some useful hints about planning a survey are given in Annex 2.

Presentation of information

Irrespective of the approach used to gather data, the usefulness of the data depends to a large extent on the way in which they are reported. Simple tabulation of the results will be adequate for some purposes, but when discussing results with key individuals or groups an attempt should be made to present the data in a way that is vivid and memorable. Consider, for example, the data concerning drugs used by the inmates of two prisons in different communities, shown in Table 2.

Table 2. Number of prison inmates using a drug almost daily

	Opium	Heroin	Cannabis	Cocaine	Solvent	Amfet-amines
Community 1 (N = 300)	54	249	42	0	78	4
Community 2 (N = 578)	23	256	20	3	0	3

The figures do not show, at a glance, the differences between the two communities. When the data are transformed into a histogram showing percentages, it is very clear which drugs and which prison community should be a cause for concern (Fig. 1).

Information is collected in order to inform. This objective is more likely to be achieved when the information is presented clearly and vividly. Exaggeration must be avoided. The aim is simply to present a clear and memorable image, in addition to the statistics. Here are a few examples:

- Within district X, 110 people die every year from illnesses and accidents related to drug and alcohol abuse. Deaths occur in all age groups. *This number of deaths is equivalent to the combined populations of two typical villages, such as Dhoba and Kandi.*
- Within the whole country, more than 100 000 people die every year from illnesses and accidents related to drug abuse. *This is the equivalent of one jumbo jet crashing every day throughout the year.*
- *On one day last month, a primary health care worker came across two families whose lives were being ruined by drug abuse. In the first, the mother was smoking opium and the small children were not being cared for. In the second, the father was*

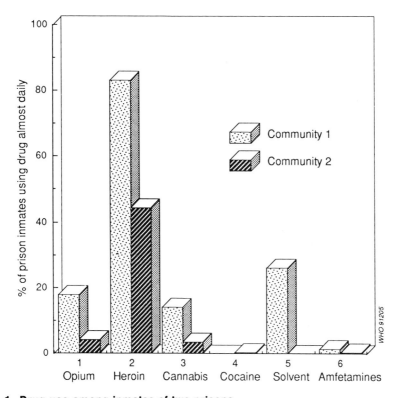

Fig. 1. Drug use among inmates of two prisons.

drinking heavily and frequently abusing his wife and children. Within this small district, there are 320 families with children, and we know of 30 who need help for a drug abuse problem. These 30 families involve 120 people.

It is important to point out also the limitations of the data, and to explain that the information represents the best estimate. You might decide to present a conservative and cautious picture, and explain that the real problem is almost certainly much worse.

Final comments

Assessment is often a difficult and time-consuming exercise. Furthermore, most of the data that can be assembled by a community action team (see Chapter 4) will have their limitations. The commonest sources of information will probably be as follows:

- self-report surveys of users,
- observations of users,
- official registration and notification records,
- studies of high-risk groups,
- hospital, clinic and emergency service admissions,
- arrest and conviction records,
- social and welfare agency records,
- production and seizure records.

All of these sources can provide useful information, but they all have their own limitations. Some of the sources concern specific groups, and do not allow easy generalization to other groups or the wider community. Clinic patients are a self-selected population and are not representative of the community. Where drug use is illegal, it might not be reported by the user unless total confidentiality is guaranteed. High turn-over of staff may create serious difficulties for systematic data collection, unless continuous training of staff is given a high priority. Despite these shortcomings, data from a variety of sources can provide an approximate estimate of the size of the problem. The more attention is paid to assessment, the better it will be.

Finally, it is important to emphasize the wealth of information and ideas that can be provided by the individual drug and alcohol abusers. First, it is possible to get a picture of the way in which a habit develops, and of the various psychological and social factors involved. Secondly, the drug user will be in a position to provide suggestions about prevention. Finally, drug users tend to have credibility with other drug users. Where possible their help and support should be sought.

3. Organizing primary health care services to combat drug and alcohol abuse

A number of principles must be borne in mind when health services are being developed to deal with drug- and alcohol-related problems in the community:

- Medical science and technology are appropriate for treating individual diseases, but are not sufficient to reduce and prevent drug- and alcohol-related problems.
- Drug- and alcohol-related problems have to be dealt with through primary health care, with emphasis on decentralized care for the promotion of health and the prevention of disease, active participation of the family and community, use of non-specialized primary health care workers, and collaboration with personnel in other governmental and nongovernmental sectors.
- The whole health sector should be structured to support decentralization, through delegation of knowledge and skills to primary health care workers and to the people themselves, to promote health for all and general well-being.
- Mental health care and the skills to deal with drug- and alcohol-related problems should be essential components of primary health care, carried out in the course of everyday activities.
- Primary health care workers should be trained in simple but effective techniques to combat drug- and alcohol-related problems, including mobilizing community action, stimulating self-help groups, providing health education, and encouraging healthy life-styles. They should be trained in skills such as interviewing, counselling, maintaining social support, crisis intervention, and providing guidance about the use of leisure time.

Functions of primary health care services

The functions of the primary health care service in relation to drug and alcohol abuse can be considered within a framework of three levels of prevention:

> **Primary prevention** aims to avoid the appearance of new cases of drug and alcohol abuse, by reducing the consumption of drugs and alcohol through health promotion.
>
> **Secondary prevention** attempts to detect cases early, and to treat them before serious complications cause disability.
>
> **Tertiary prevention** aims to avoid further disabilities, and to reintegrate into society individuals who have been harmed by severe drug and alcohol problems.

The PHC worker will be involved at all of these levels.

Primary prevention

The primary health care service is in a position to meet people's needs and to deliver health care to individuals or families at their homes or workplaces. It would be quite unrealistic to expect the primary health care worker to develop complex or specialized activities. However, the PHC worker can provide a very cost-effective service by using relatively simple skills of listening, communication, and counselling. In order to develop primary health care services directed towards drug and alcohol problems, PHC workers will have to undertake the interrelated activities described below.

Identify drugs currently used in the community

The PHC worker should learn about the drugs in use locally, as well as the consequences of excessive use. It must be emphasized that information has to be quite detailed. It may be, for example, that a local home brew is mixed with cheap alcohols that are extremely toxic.

Identify the ways in which drugs and alcohol are used in the community

The ways in which drugs are used in a community tend to change frequently. Minor tranquillizers might be used secretly by certain groups, who buy them from a friendly pharmacist or get them through medical prescriptions. Alcohol is supplied without restrictions in many countries, but it will not be easy to find the places where very young children drink cheap alcoholic beverages. There may also be open-air places where children meet to sniff gasoline or glue, under the guise of playing or chatting.

Teenagers and young adults use drugs, or combinations of drugs, according to the fashion. It is also important to detect any intravenous use of drugs, because of the associated infections.

Information and education to promote health

PHC workers are in a position to disseminate relevant information on drugs and alcohol to the community. They can put up posters in the places where most people are likely to see them. They can also distribute reading matter to special groups or organizations, such as parents' organizations. Finally, PHC workers might be invited to conferences on drug- and alcohol-related problems in schools, sporting associations, mothers' clubs, etc. More important than information dissemination is the education of people through a two-way process of communication and interaction. For example, it is quite natural to talk about drug and alcohol problems with pregnant women or young mothers. Most of the time, it will be possible to educate people about the prevention of drug and alcohol abuse without specifying that there is a special programme to combat such problems.

Integrating primary health care work with that of other groups

The PHC worker should work with groups, such as schoolteachers, police, district commissioners, churches, clubs, volunteers, and traditional healers. If the PHC worker is able to develop good interpersonal and leadership skills, he or she will find it much easier to mobilize the community and organize specific voluntary groups to deal with drug- and alcohol-related problems.

Secondary prevention

Identify the immediate effects of drug and alcohol abuse

As the ways of taking drugs change, so do their effects. Whether a drug is harmful or not depends upon the following factors:

- the user: his or her nutrition, other diseases, etc.
- the drug: its purity, dosage, combination with other drugs, etc.
- the environment: for example, the influence of children who sniff glue together, prisoners who learn to inject heroin, young students who drink at weekend parties.

The effects will be different when drugs are taken in combination: for example, it has become a common practice in Andean cities to smoke, or sniff, cocaine in order to reverse the effects of alcohol, and to drink alcohol to control anxiety or paranoia provoked by cocaine use. Some people may react very badly even to small quantities of drugs and alcohol; on the other hand, tolerant and dependent abusers are often able to take enormous quantities without showing signs of intoxication.

Identify harmful use and high-risk groups

With some drugs and alcohol, it is often difficult to draw a line between safe and harmful use. For example, to drink 1 or 2 litres of beer may be relatively safe, but this amount could become harmful if taken daily for several years. Celebrating the New Year with three or four drinks could be extremely dangerous if the drinker drives afterwards. Some people stand a very high risk of harming themselves, or others, if they use drugs or alcohol: for example, pregnant women, car drivers, people operating machinery, and those who already have a serious drug- or alcohol-related

Drinking and driving are a dangerous combination.

32

problem. Others at risk include those with a mental illness or taking medication. Use of illegal drugs is almost always harmful, not only because of the threat to health, but also because of the potential social, legal, and economic consequences. A brief intervention can be very useful with a person in a high-risk group. Such brief interventions are dealt with in Chapter 5 of this manual, and might involve a discussion of the benefits of reducing consumption, as well as of ways of coping without the drug or alcohol.

Tertiary prevention

Identify and manage patients with acute conditions that must be treated without delay

Some acute conditions related to drug and alcohol abuse appear suddenly as emergency problems. The most dramatic are delirium tremens, epileptic fits, confused or agitated behaviour, paranoia, suicide attempts, and the taking of an overdose. When faced with any of these life-threatening conditions, the PHC worker may need to give emergency medication; he or she will therefore need appropriate training and close links with specialist workers.

Identify and manage patients with drug and alcohol problems who must be referred to other services

Some conditions associated with drug and alcohol abuse should ideally be handled in a hospital; for example, epilepsy, liver cirrhosis, peptic ulcer, lung infections, acquired immunodeficiency syndrome (AIDS), hepatitis. There are also some psychiatric conditions that should be referred to a specialist service, and some patients requiring detoxification who should be seen by a hospital service. The PHC worker has to learn which patients to refer, and to whom.

Identify and alleviate family problems related to drugs and alcohol

Besides damaging the brain and the body, drugs and alcohol modify the functioning and control of emotions, desires, thoughts, and perceptions, and also disrupt social and family relationships. The patient may be alienated from all social contact, a vicious circle being established with the patient becoming more and more hostile, and the family more and more unresponsive. Jealousy, violence, unusual patterns of eating and sleeping, fears of being poisoned, and so on, may provoke adverse reactions in other

33

members of the family. The PHC worker should be able to question family members about these problems, and help them to cope with the emotional turmoil. Chapter 5 covers simple interventions to help families deal with problems and cope with crises.

Helping social rehabilitation

Former drug abusers are fragile beings who have passed through a difficult stage. They need help to readjust to social life and its constraints. The PHC worker should attempt to improve the social relationships of former drug and alcohol abusers, and perhaps introduce them to community self-help and voluntary groups.

Functions of the second level of health care

The second level of health care is usually based at a district hospital. The hospital is staffed by specialists in a range of areas who will see patients suffering from the consequences of drug and alcohol abuse. Registered nurses, social workers, and administrators will all have to deal with such patients. Some training will be necessary for these personnel, so that they can use their knowledge and skills to develop a service to deal with drug- and alcohol-related problems. The functions of this service are described below.

Treating patients referred from primary care

The characteristics of patients vary from one community to another, according to the drugs used, and to their background. Sometimes, guidelines for treating the most common clinical conditions are useful. As an illustration, Table 3 provides an outline of a treatment programme for alcohol withdrawal symptoms in severely dependent patients.

Referral back to primary level

Recovered patients should be sent back to the PHC worker with clear, written indications as regards:

- diagnosis (somatic, neurological, and psychiatric), with comments on expected risks and complications;
- treatment given in the hospital, and the maintenance medication that has to be continued at home, specifying the doses and any expected side-effects;

Table 3. Treatment of alcohol-related syndromes in hospital

Syndrome	Expected complications	Suggested investigations and treatment
Dependence	Withdrawal symptoms	• Mild sedatives (chlordiazepoxide 20 mg orally, 3 times daily) • Vitamin B complex (1 tablet, 3 times daily) • Careful physical, neurological, and psychiatric examination • Laboratory tests: blood, liver, urine • If no complications: discharge in 10 days
Delirium tremens	Epileptic fit Fever Pneumonia Death	• Diazepam (10 mg, intravenously, every 6 hours) • Vitamin B1, thiamine, intramuscularly, every 12 hours • Glucose and saline solutions, 2000 ml, intravenously, every 24 hours • Check temperature, state of consciousness, every 3 hours • Antibiotics if necessary • Complete physical examination. Do not discharge before 15 days.
Alcoholic coma	Fractured skull Subdural haematoma Bronchial aspiration Death	• X-rays: skull, lungs • Laboratory tests: blood, lumbar tap • Check vital signs and reflexes every hour

- suggestions for psychosocial interventions, especially ways of supporting or influencing the family;
- indications for future referral, if necessary.

Supplying essential medication

Workers at the primary care level need to have a stock of essential medicines and to know how to use them. Some of these medications must be taken by patients regularly for long periods (e.g., anticonvulsive pills). Other medications have to be given for only a few weeks (e.g., antidepressants, after a suicide attempt). Finally, some medications are necessary for treating emergencies (e.g., chlorpromazine for paranoid agitation induced by cocaine). Second-level personnel should train PHC workers in the administration of these medications and the prevention of side-effects, as well as in the maintenance of the stock of medicines.

Training PHC workers

First-level health care personnel will usually receive practical training at the district hospital; supervising this training is a key function of the professionals in the hospital. They should also pay frequent and regular visits to primary health care services for the purposes of supervision and consultation.

The changing role of specialists

The role of specialist psychologists, psychiatrists, social workers, and other professionals in a decentralized system is to support the primary health care service by carrying out the following functions:

- They act as educators and agents of social change for the health and other sectors, with regard to drug- and alcohol-related problems, and should attempt to stimulate public awareness of the situation.
- They are consultants for the most difficult cases referred from the primary level; they should avoid being inundated with individual patients who can be dealt with by less qualified staff members.
- They should visit primary health care facilities on a regular basis as consultants and supervisors, and should encourage preventive and curative interventions, as well as simple research.
- They should decide upon the skills and knowledge to be transferred to the lower levels of the service, and prepare the schedules for in-service training.
- They should coordinate and evaluate the whole system, analysing the information collected, and disseminating the results as appropriate.

PHC workers should have a stock of essential medicines.

● They should participate in the development and monitoring of national policies and programmes, particularly those aspects related to financial support and to the employment and placement of former dependent persons.
● They should act as advocates to generate public support and advise local and national authorities, the heads of other sectors, and the mass media on matters related to drugs and alcohol.

New role for the specialist

● Educate, facilitate, and stimulate
● Consult on difficult cases
● Support and motivate PHC workers
● Transfer skills
● Coordinate and evaluate
● Plan and monitor national policies
● Become advocate and advisor.

Coordination with other sectors

To ensure coordination between the various sectors involved, it will be useful to form a community action team (CAT) with representatives from health and other sectors. The members of these teams should be drawn from sectors and groups with a stake in community development. CAT members should be in close contact with members of the community, seeking answers to questions such as:

● What does the community identify as its drug and alcohol problems?
● Who is vulnerable in the community?
● What does the community believe should be done?

The CAT should collect background information on social definitions, perceptions, and responses connected with drug and alcohol problems, as well as on attitudes and the degree of awareness regarding drinking habits and drug use.

It is important that, in all of this, the PHC workers should not see themselves as lone individuals seeking to involve the community. Partnership between health workers, government agencies, social services, and voluntary groups is vital in dealing with drug- and alcohol-related problems in the community. Such problems can never be adequately managed by one person, or sector, working in isolation.

The CAT should coordinate the actions of various interested parties, including health professionals and associations, researchers, law-makers, law-enforcement agents, educators, and community groups, such as women's and youth organizations and churches. Strategies and decisions to develop drug and alcohol programmes should be negotiated by the CAT, or other community committees, which should function at all levels of the health system.

Intersectoral collaboration might also be established using the "gate-keeper" approach; this involves, first, finding out from other sector personnel what they need to know in order to decide whether to collaborate with a health programme. This step stimulates the initial interest. The next move is to find the information they require and pass it on to the other sector, which will then be more likely to act.

Government agencies are usually organized vertically, with representation at all levels but, because of their bureaucratic structure, they often do not develop horizontal collaboration. On the other hand, nongovernmental organizations may be preoccupied with managing their budgets and are often reluctant to develop a partnership for fear of losing their freedom of action. Despite these barriers, the potential of other sectors should be tapped, using the "gatekeeper" technique or another approach, to support drug and alcohol programmes at the community level. Negative attitudes need to be changed across all sectors.

WHO 91189

The CAT should coordinate the activities of the various interested parties.

Intersectoral collaboration should be a constant process that must be kept alive by the CAT; the team should organize regular meetings, interactions, and task assignments with community representatives, anticipating as far as possible any likely obstacles and problems.

Evaluation and monitoring

If services for dealing with drug- and alcohol-related problems are organized according to the principles mentioned on page 29—that is to say, decentralized services, with active participation of the community, and undertaken by nonspecialized health workers—it will be important to demonstrate their effectiveness in achieving targets, as well as their efficiency in the use of resources. In addition, health workers, especially those who are not specialized and who work at the community level, need to keep track of what they are doing through feedback from supervisors.

In order to meet these needs, a process of data collection and monitoring is required. Data must be relevant to the everyday work of the PHC worker, and the source of information should be the individual health workers.

Personal contact in the transfer of information is important in order to clarify the relevance of the data, reinforce the motivation for data collection, and give timely feedback. This process can become the basis for continuing in-service training and support for the PHC worker.

Indicators of these activities or of the performance of a team have to be clear and simple. Examples are:

- number of cases per week, and the types of drugs used;
- frequency of visits to families and individuals;
- proportion of cases referred;
- number of contacts with other sectors;
- number of people identified as being at risk;
- number of meetings with self-help groups;
- type and quantity of medications used.

It is also necessary to assess the service and the programme, and to evaluate its management and its relevance to the needs of the community. Information for this evaluation is not always quantitative. Sometimes it will be necessary to carry out formal research. Such research undertakings need not be expensive and can be done as part of a training programme for health workers.

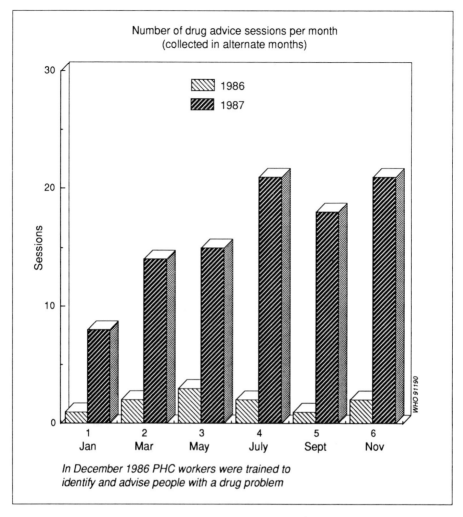

Number of drug advice sessions per month
(collected in alternate months)

In December 1986 PHC workers were trained to
identify and advise people with a drug problem

Indicators should be clear and simple, and related to the targets of the programme.

Information on the way in which services operate should be simple and relevant to possible improvements. Such information could be collected by asking questions such as:

- Is there a logical structure for referral and supervision?
- What mechanisms are used to engage other sectors?
- Are drug and alcohol abusers helped in peripheral centres and in the community?
- Are there registries and systems for data collection?
- Does a community action team meet regularly?

Other types of indicator will be needed to show the impact of the programme and its advantages, as reflected in savings in other areas, for example:

- reduction in re-admission rates;
- savings in costs of specialized hospital treatment;
- reductions in incidence and prevalence of drug- and alcohol-related problems.

All this must be accomplished with continuing support and discussion, so that the health workers understand the relevance of the data collection and monitoring.

Training

Training is at the core of decentralization. The delegation of skills and functions means that nonspecialized personnel need to be trained to deliver health care at the peripheral centres and within families and homes. Most of the training should be based on an apprenticeship system, using the attitudes and behaviour of senior personnel and professionals as models. Traditionally, psychosocial and interpersonal skills have been regarded as either inherent and intuitive, or acquired only after a long period of trial and error. This supposition is wrong and needs to be changed.

Effective delegation of skills can be achieved through direct practical training, using a variety of teaching methods, e.g., small group discussions, supervised in-service work, and imitative learning. Essential skills to be taught include:

- interviewing skills;
- ability to listen and to be empathic;
- interpersonal skills needed for counselling, guiding and persuading;
- relaxation, meditation, and culture-specific skills, such as acupuncture, prayer, hypnotism, incantation, and the use of medicinal herbs;
- the management of essential medications;
- the detection of behavioural symptoms;
- a complete approach to problems, incorporating biological, psychological, and sociological points of view;
- recognition of the importance of working with other people in the community, outside the health sector;
- ability to understand and deal with local community fears, beliefs, taboos and attitudes.

The learning of these skills is different from the process of acquiring information and psychomotor skills; it depends on having examples to imitate, and on frank discussion of what is being done. The aim is to change attitudes by constantly reinforcing positive opinions and points of view. These attitudinal and behavioural changes have to be instilled and shaped from the very beginning of training and continually reinforced.

Budget

Services will operate effectively only if the resources are appropriately assigned. This does not imply extensive financial outlay. On the contrary, an effective alcohol and drug service can reduce overall health costs.

Drug and alcohol services do not demand expensive methods, but rather the deployment of simple skills to the primary health care workers, broadening their approach, and improving their efficiency. The following activities will need to be funded:

- training activities;
- supervision and support from higher levels;
- appropriate means of transport;
- support of coordinating groups (most of them voluntary), e.g., the CAT;
- provision of essential medication;
- establishment of key, multidisciplinary staff members, such as a co-ordinator or community nurse.

In summary, the primary health care worker deals with drug and alcohol problems within the primary health care setting, but works within the wider community and looks to the hospital specialist for support. This may appear to be too much work for a primary level worker. It should be remembered, however, that the system described here is an ideal to be worked towards. The PHC worker should attempt to obtain help from both the community and specialist workers to work out effective ways of providing a primary health care alcohol and drug service within the community.

4. Mobilizing the community to reduce drug and alcohol abuse

This chapter is concerned with the task of mobilizing the whole community to take coordinated action to prevent drug and alcohol abuse. In a recent innovative programme in Pakistan, for example, village health committees worked in close liaison with a medical practitioner to develop just such a community response. The village committees consisted of influential and enthusiastic people who could make sure that changes occurred. These people were given training in the early detection, referral, and rehabilitation of drug users in their localities. Also, working in close collaboration with schoolteachers and students, they placed a great deal of emphasis on health education. This kind of active liaison between groups or organizations must be encouraged if the recent worldwide escalation in the problem of alcohol and drug abuse is to be reversed.

The need to mobilize communities

The use of psychoactive substances is a phenomenon with which all communities and countries have regular acquaintance. Some drugs are illegal but others with abuse potential are sanctioned for use in religious rituals, community ceremonies, and leisure-time activities. Although these socially acceptable drugs are in everyday use, they almost certainly result in some harmful consequences.

Whenever a new drug appears on the scene, it becomes a matter of some concern, particularly if it affects the young and the economically productive adults, or becomes symbolically associated with changes in social norms and values. This concern leads to many kinds of community response, which, if properly channelled, can form the basis for a community action programme. It is, however, a much more difficult task to persuade a community that there are good reasons to be worried about substances that have been traditionally used for ceremonial and recreational use (e.g., tobacco, alcohol, raw opium, cannabis products, khat, and coca). The community may have failed to recognize the harmful potential of these drugs, or may have decided simply to accept the consequences. In these circumstances, changes in behaviour can only be brought about and sustained if the community becomes actively involved in promoting good health.

The community action team

Although the primary health care worker should aim to play a key role in nudging a community towards healthier attitudes and life-styles, there is no doubt that external help will be required, right from the start. For example, one of the most difficult, but necessary and interesting, tasks is to build up a clear picture of the community. This should include not only some information on the drugs that are used and abused, but much more besides, including answers to some of the following questions:

- Which organizations make important decisions?
- Who are the key individuals in the community?
- How are plans and concerns communicated or disseminated?
- How are the price and availability of drugs determined?
- What legislation is involved and how is it enforced?
- Which professional and voluntary workers are interested or could be persuaded to take an interest in drug abuse?
- Which other individuals or groups could help or have some influence?

To facilitate the collection of this type of information, a community action team (CAT) should be formed with representatives of the health sector, the police, business, social services, voluntary bodies, parents, teachers, and any other groups or organizations with an interest in preventing drug and alcohol abuse and related problems. The first task of this team will be to collect a wide range of background information.

Background information

Chapter 2 provides guidelines on how to assess drug-related problems within a community. This chapter should be consulted before any attempt is made to build up a file of useful information.

Evidence and information should be collected and collated in the following six subject areas.

How is the community organized?

Even within a small area, communities have their similarities and differences. Some village communities have a hierarchical structure, whereas others are more democratic. There will be differences between rural and urban societies, and different types of groups will co-exist within a particular community. There will be various pressure groups, as well as formal and informal associations involved in a wide range of areas, such as agricultural development, education, women's concerns, parent–teacher activities, and labour unions.

It is important to understand how the individuals and the groups relate to each other, how the community leaders lead, and what communication styles they use. The interactions in a hierarchical rural society are probably different from those in urban areas. Even within a hierarchical rural society, the village headman, or tribal chief, may have absolute authority to settle certain issues, e.g., disputes about land, marriages, and economic rights, while the authority on other issues, such as drug abuse, may be exercised by some other person or group.

A clear picture of the leadership and communication patterns within a community is an invaluable asset to the PHC worker and the community action team. An ability to plug into the correct communication channels and to influence opinion leaders and decision-makers is vital to any community action programme.

What are the customary methods of problem-solving and decision-making?

Communities have their own methods of solving problems and making decisions about issues of common concern to their members. In some rural societies, this could involve a discussion of the problem by an informal group, or a committee, under the leadership of an elected or traditional leader. The decision might then be binding for the rest of the community. In urban societies, problems might be discussed by an elected community welfare group (e.g., the residents' welfare association) or a recognized formal association (e.g., the employees' union). The community action team should attempt to negotiate with these key decision-making groups in order to get the issue of substance abuse on to their agendas and to obtain an appropriate response. This can only be achieved if the appropriate groups are approached in an acceptable way.

If the action team wishes to increase drug education in schools, who should they approach—the education minister, parent–teacher associations, headmasters, or a group advising the minister on the content of the school curriculum? Which groups or individuals have a vested interest in

45

preventing accidents resulting from drug and alcohol abuse? This type of information is as important as information about the prevalence and nature of drug abuse within a community.

What are the major drug- and alcohol-related problems?

Chapter 2 outlines ways of exploring the problems resulting from drug abuse within a particular area. Evidence of local substance-related problems, when clearly and vividly presented, can be very useful in encouraging a community to regulate itself. Evidence, such as the following, speaks for itself:

- "Over 30% of drivers killed in road accidents have high blood alcohol levels. On Saturday nights this figure rises to 70%."
- "Over 30% of those requesting help from primary health care workers and social workers are abusing drugs and/or alcohol."
- "Drugs and/or alcohol are implicated in 40% of family disputes involving the police."
- "Over 90% of people dying from lung cancer are smokers."

Evidence of this type is not always readily available for a particular community, and evidence from other sources may have to be used.

What community programmes already exist?

Within the community health service, there will be programmes and services that already have to cope with drug-related illness. It is important to identify these and to start a dialogue with the following aims in mind: first, to convince health service managers and clinical teams that drug and alcohol abuse should be given a high priority; secondly, to encourage key individuals to participate either in the CAT or in specific programmes; thirdly, to discuss the possibility that materials, resources, and funding might be assigned to the CAT.

Of course, the health service is not the only sector involved in health-related programmes. Organizations responsible for education, housing, safety, nutrition, policing, and leisure might already have an interest in drug and alcohol abuse. If not, they should be encouraged to develop an interest. Furthermore, most communities have a number of voluntary organizations that are very active and influential (e.g., Rotary Clubs, youth clubs, study circles, and women's groups). When collecting background information about all of these groups and organizations, it is important to discover (*a*) who are the key decision-makers, and (*b*) how they should be approached for support. If you know what motivates the chief of police, then you will know how to present your proposal to him or her.

What existing legislation relates to drug abuse?

Within most communities, there will be legislation relating to substance abuse. Most countries have laws derived from the Single Convention on Narcotic Drugs (1961) and the International Convention on Psychotropic Substances (1971). Such legislation usually has a built-in component to deal with treatment and rehabilitation (e.g., compulsory treatment, legally designated treatment centres, rehabilitation programmes). Information on such legislation may be available from the police or district health authority.

The CAT should also be aware of other legislation directed towards tobacco and alcoholic beverages (e.g., concerning health warnings). There may be laws relating to home-brewed alcoholic beverages, quantities of alcoholic beverage that individuals may possess for consumption, age restrictions on the sale and consumption of alcohol, designated places of consumption, and restrictions on drinking and driving. This information may be available from the alcohol licensing authority or the police.

There will also be legislation and penalties governing the sale and possession of opiates for medicinal uses, and of other psychoactive drugs that are controlled by prescription (e.g., barbiturates, amfetamines, benzodiazepines). The pharmacist, the drug control administration, and the district health administrators should be able to provide this type of information.

How can the CAT get the message to the community?

Most communities have a local newspaper or news sheet. Many have more than one, as well as other forms of communication (e.g., radio, TV). A very important component of the CAT's work is to raise the community's level of awareness about drug and alcohol problems and programmes. This will involve patiently developing a strong relationship with key individuals with access to communication channels. Who are these people? Are they interested in health issues? Will they run a campaign? Can they help to develop materials (e.g., leaflets)?

A journalist, or a media representative, will often be a very useful and helpful member of the community action team.

47

It is important to get the messages across to the community.

Developing and implementing a community drug and alcohol strategy

Having formed a CAT and collected background information on the extent of substance abuse, and on the key groups and decision-makers, the next stage is to use all this information to develop plans. In moving on to this stage, the following basic principles should be borne in mind.

● **Negotiate, don't dictate**. When attempting to change established beliefs, it is wise to look for areas of agreement or common agendas. For example, if a school or sports club is concerned with "fitness through exercise", it should not be too difficult to discuss a drug programme within the same framework. The owner of a bar is in business to make a profit. Encouraging the sale of low-alcohol beers should help profits and also reduce drink-driving accidents.

48

- **Aim for small successes**. Don't worry too much about the daunting prospect of developing a large, comprehensive, community drug and alcohol strategy that addresses all the issues, in all age groups and all sectors of the community. Instead go for smaller-scale objectives that stand a good chance of succeeding. Put an article in the local newspaper. Persuade a police officer to start a drink-driving campaign. One small success tends to lead to other small successes. Small successes are good for morale. Furthermore, they attract support, and sometimes resources and funds. Whenever possible, ensure that one key worker has responsibility for a particular project, since diffusion of responsibility can lead to chaos.
- **Encourage community participation at each stage.** Annex 3 gives a checklist of questions that can guide the development of a community programme. A programme that does not have local support and community involvement will quickly grind to a halt.

The rest of this chapter describes a number of actions that may or may not be relevant to a particular community. They are given here simply as examples.

Developing an information base

The CAT should be in a position to use information derived from the community assessment. These data may show, roughly, the numbers of individuals who abuse a given type of substance. They might also indicate some of the adverse health and social consequences, e.g., loss of weight related to a drug habit, repeated chest infections, suicide attempts and accidental overdoses, poisoning, family discord and violence, loss of family assets, petty crime and theft.

In addition, some information might be available about existing programmes, including those directed towards treatment, rehabilitation, and continuing care. Having assembled all this information, the primary health care worker, or other member of the CAT, is in a very good position to serve as an information resource for the community. The CAT might consider publishing a booklet entitled *Dealing with drug abuse in Kandi,* or something similar, covering the extent of the problem, the consequences of drug and alcohol abuse, and suggested strategies for various groups and organizations.

Raising awareness

Publicizing and disseminating a booklet on dealing with substance abuse could mark the launch of a programme or campaign. Discuss such an initiative with the local newspaper or radio, well in advance of publication, so that the dissemination of information is planned and not fortuitous. If you have a lot of information, you could hold back some of it for future publicity events or newspaper articles. The best strategy is to remind the community about drug abuse at regular intervals, but not so frequently that people become bored, and the campaign loses its impact.

Publicity events should be as vivid and as memorable as possible. With the cooperation of a school, arrange for a group of children to dramatize the number of people who will die prematurely as a result of use of alcohol, drugs, or tobacco. Ask a local drama group to act out a number of brief stories involving the consequences of drug abuse (e.g., drinking and driving, violence within the family). If possible, persuade a well-known person to lead the campaign.

Members of the CAT, or other interested individuals, could be encouraged to address various community groups, e.g., the women's institute, parent–teacher associations, youth clubs.

Integration with other programmes

Most people are concerned about their health and well-being. When they visit a doctor, community health worker, or pharmacist, they are usually ready to listen to advice; health workers should therefore take the opportunity to discuss drug abuse. They should ask routinely about drug use, and provide advice about changing life-style and obtaining further help. Early identification and early intervention are discussed in Chapters 1 and 5, but the most important first step is for the health worker to be continuously vigilant. Problems as diverse as depression, nausea, and family disputes might well be linked to drug abuse.

The pharmacist is one of the local experts on drugs, and will usually be a supportive member of the CAT. Leaflets and advice distributed by the pharmacist might be one way to disseminate information.

In Zimbabwe (as in many countries), the occupational health nurse is well placed to identify drug and alcohol problems at an early stage. In one project, the nurse regularly asks questions about substance abuse, and looks out for signs of possible abuse, such as "Monday-morning" symptoms, accidents, disputes at work, and absenteeism after pay-days. The occupational nurse gives advice where necessary, and makes a home visit if this seems warranted. If all primary health care workers followed this model, and also obtained help from others, a great deal could be done to prevent the escalation of the substance abuse problem.

Alcohol and drug policies for organizations

A great deal of drug and alcohol use occurs in the work environment. Organizations and businesses should be encouraged to develop a policy relating to drug and alcohol use, focused upon health and safety at work. Here are a few examples:

- If alcohol is served on the premises, there should also be cheap non-alcoholic beverages, so that a choice is offered.
- Employees using complex machinery should not drink or use drugs while at work.
- Employees with a poor work record, resulting from a drug or alcohol problem, should be offered counselling as a first step.
- Smoking should be allowed only in certain designated places, since nonsmokers have the right to work in a smoke-free atmosphere.

Developing a drug and alcohol policy is an excellent method of raising awareness. It is particularly important that members of the health service provide an example for the rest of the community to follow.

Self-help approaches

Fifty years ago in the United States of America, two alcohol-dependent people concluded that they could not conquer their problem alone, but that they might be able to beat it together. Their success led to the worldwide movement now known as Alcoholics Anonymous. Working on a problem in a group has a number of clear advantages. First, understanding and support are provided by others with a similar problem. Secondly, those who are coping successfully can pass on helpful advice. Also, when attempting to solve a problem, two heads are usually better than one. Finally, some people find that they get a great deal of satisfaction from giving help to others.

In Hong Kong, the Alumni Association of Sarda is a self-help organization composed of, and managed by, former drug-dependent people. Following detoxification and rehabilitation, former addicts are welcomed back into the community by the group, which arranges support and after-care in liaison with health and social services.

A self-help group can be started by three or four enthusiastic people who feel that they would like to give and get help. They could be drug abusers, recovering drug abusers, or members of their families. Self-help groups can provide valuable support to the community action team.

Developing a youth programme

Drug use often begins during adolescence. Perhaps the most effective method of dealing with the drug abuse problem in a community is to prevent the habit developing in the first place. There are a number of ways of educating and influencing young people, including the following:

- Education about the harmful effects of drugs should be included in the basic school curriculum, either as a separate course or as part of other courses (e.g., biology, health care).
- One method of consolidating this teaching is to ask a class to design a set of posters warning about the dangers of drug abuse. A group, such as the local Rotary Club, might be persuaded to run a poster competition and present prizes.
- A group of young people could be encouraged to develop a "youth-link" network of youth groups that are interested in preventing drug and alcohol abuse. Such groups could be linked to the CAT, but they should be encouraged to implement ideas and programmes developed by young people for young people.

This youth programme would be one distinct component of the community response, and as such should be managed and monitored by one person—perhaps a teacher, a parent, or a young person.

Law enforcement

The community action team should develop a close relationship with law enforcement agencies, since the CAT and the police certainly have common concerns that can be explored jointly. For example, in many communities the purchase of alcohol and cigarettes by children is a major concern. How can the police help to solve this problem? How can the law enforcement agencies influence drug availability? In districts where community policing is considered to be an effective crime prevention strategy, a great deal can be accomplished. For example, in some societies it is illegal to serve drinks to people who are already intoxicated, and to those who are under a certain age. In one study carried out in the United Kingdom, a 20% reduction in crime was achieved when the police regularly reminded bar staff of these laws, and paid visits to particular bars to ensure that the laws were being observed.

The police usually come into contact with drug abusers and their families, and could serve as a channel of communication to disseminate information about sources of help and advice.

Accident prevention

In many societies, accidents are a major cause of death in young and old people. Because large numbers of young people are involved, accidents are usually the events that result in the greatest number of lost years of life. Since drugs and alcohol are usually implicated in more than 30% of accidents on the roads, in the home, and at work, an accident prevention campaign is an excellent way to start a campaign to prevent drug abuse.

One great advantage of such a campaign is that it is likely to be non-controversial. An accident prevention group could include brewers, bar staff, the police, public transport, and young people, as well as the health and social services. An accident prevention campaign will be well received by most community groups, and is a good method of developing a nucleus of concerned people. This nucleus could then become involved with other activities aimed at preventing drug abuse. The focus on accidents serves as a point of entry into the networks involved in decision-making and the process of change.

Monitoring and evaluation

It is important that the CAT obtains as much feedback as possible about developments and achievements, since knowledge of results is the only way to ensure that the programme is proceeding in the right direction. If a particular programme is failing, it must be modified. On the other hand, knowledge of successes keeps motivation high and encourages everybody involved to keep up the good work.

When trying to keep track of community action, it might be helpful to think of three types of information:

- **Inputs.** What actions are taken by the CAT? For example, discuss drug education with the local head teacher and the parent–teacher association; persuade the Rotary Club to be involved.
- **Processes.** What chain of events follows from these activities? For example, one teacher volunteered to run a poster campaign; winners' names were published in the newspaper; the Rotary Club paid for the printing and distribution of the winning poster.
- **Outcome.** As a result of all the inputs and processes, what objectives have been achieved? For example, is it possible to identify changes in the occurrence of accidents or the crime rate; do children know more about drug abuse?

Some of the information needed to monitor the programme can be provided by members of the CAT, or by the wider group of people involved in the project. Outcome information will also have to be collated from a variety of official sources; and if a community survey has been carried out, it can perhaps be repeated.

The CAT should delegate overall responsibility for monitoring to one person, and regular meetings should be held in order to keep track of relevant information and feedback.

Final comments

Drug abuse is a problem that is either stigmatized and considered to be unacceptable, or accepted as a leisure and recreational activity. Both of these attitudes can persuade a community that no action needs to be taken. Furthermore, with alcohol and cigarettes, it is sometimes argued that drug users are free to abuse themselves if they want to. These attitudes should not be confronted directly, but common agendas should be identified (e.g., Is heroin abuse draining health service resources? Are smokers polluting the office environment?). In addition to society's ambivalence about drug abuse, many vested interests will be involved. These should be identified by the CAT.

A community has only limited energy and resources to direct towards the problem of drug abuse. In order to harness this energy and attract resources, the CAT must be persuasive and enthusiastic. Small successes can generate a great deal of enthusiasm.

Finally, it should be noted that members of a community action team should look towards their own use of drugs before they try to influence the community. Changing your life-style or that of the community is a difficult but rewarding task.

5. Helping the individual with drug- or alcohol-related problems

The care of individuals with drug- or alcohol-related problems is not the preserve of any one health profession or group. Medical practitioners, clinical psychologists, social workers, and other less specialized personnel all have important contributions to make. Such care does not have to be provided in an institutional setting; the role of the community health worker has been increasingly emphasized in recent years. Furthermore, the concept of health for all by the year 2000 will become a reality only if problems such as drug dependence and alcohol abuse are handled mainly through primary health care.

The aims of this chapter are to help primary health care workers to define their role in the management of people with drug- and alcohol-related problems and to equip them with the necessary skills. It is assumed that PHC workers see themselves as members of a team of health workers functioning at the community level.

It should be borne in mind that drug and alcohol dependence are often relapsing conditions. It is, therefore, unhelpful if the carer's attitude is judgemental, critical, or moralistic. The patient needs reassurance and understanding, not rebuke and rejection. The life of a drug-dependent person is usually full of crises, and carers should be able and willing to accept this state of affairs and to help the patient deal with it.

Helping a drug-dependent person

Who is a drug-dependent person? First and foremost, he or she is a human being, with feelings and emotions, capable of appreciating help. Drug-related problems may be almost totally buried inside other social, physical, and psychological problems. Furthermore, drug-dependent people may try to ignore their drug problems, even denying that they exist. This denial is a "brick wall" that drug-dependent people erect around themselves. The wall must come down, and the health worker must help to demolish it.

Behind the wall of denial there are usually a number of social, physical, and psychological problems. A female problem drinker, for example, is likely to see herself as an outcast, and others may see her in the same way. She probably spends a great deal of money to satisfy her need for alcohol and is thus relatively poor. Her family is probably embarrassed by her drinking. She may have become unemployed and is sometimes unemployable. With time she might lose her home, her family, and her self-respect. She may suffer from physical illnesses that are a direct consequence of the alcohol abuse, just as she may present with psychological problems, severe depression, anxiety, or even discrete psychiatric syndromes.

It is clear that the problems associated with drug and alcohol abuse are not always medical, but are often social and psychological in nature. Medically, there is not a single physical system in the body that remains untouched by drugs and alcohol. Most mental systems are also affected. Hallucinations and delusions occur and mood changes are very common. Socially, clients often require assistance to help them return to a semblance of normal existence. They may need help to refrain from criminal behaviour, find a home and employment, avoid activities and crises that will precipitate a relapse, and develop new relationships.

Apart from participating in activities to prevent drug and alcohol abuse and in treatment programmes, the primary health care worker has the added responsibility of identifying drug-dependent persons, and individuals with alcohol-related problems, within the community, and of ensuring that they receive treatment at an early stage.

Dealing with such a wide range of problems and activities might seem to be an overwhelming task. Remember, however, that, whenever possible, the PHC worker should obtain the support of a wider team, including volunteers and relatives of the patient. If this is not possible, the PHC worker should at least try to influence a client in the right direction.

It is useful to divide the management of drug- or alcohol-dependent persons into four distinct phases, even though these overlap. They are:

- assessment,
- detoxification,
- specialized interventions,
- follow-up and after-care.

A client may not require detoxification. As a rule, detoxification is called for only when severe withdrawal symptoms are expected to occur following a quick return to abstinence or minimal drug use.

56

Assessment

Chapter 1 deals with assessment of the individual as a preparation for action. The main aims of assessment are:

- to obtain as much accurate information as possible about the individual's drug use and any associated problems;
- to try to identify the factors associated with drug abuse in the individual—these may be physical illnesses or social or psychological factors;
- to assist the PHC worker to recognize the strengths and weaknesses of the individual and his/her family, as well as his/her ability to cope with the problems and assist in their management.

A good assessment interview will help to develop a positive, helpful relationship, and will serve to build up a picture of the client's particular problems. As a basis for action, an assessment should provide information relating to the following treatment goals:

- improving social relationships and supports;
- developing confidence in ability to change;
- identifying reasons to change;
- developing alternative activities;
- learning to prevent relapse.

One way of remembering these five goals

Remember the word **SCRAP** which stands for:
    S = social relationships
    C = confidence in ability to change
    R = reasons to change
    A = alternative activities
    P = preventing relapse

Detoxification

Of all the drug-dependent people that the PHC worker will see, those who use opiates, or excessive amounts of alcohol, are most likely to experience severe withdrawal symptoms. It is difficult to predict the severity of these symptoms, but the best evidence of what to expect is provided by a client's past experience of withdrawal.

Intense craving, and most of the physical dangers that can result from the sudden termination of a drug, can be forestalled by gradually reducing use of the drug, or by using a substitute. Gradual detoxification may take many months to complete, as is often the case when heroin is replaced by methadone, which is itself gradually withdrawn. Indeed, some therapists are happy to leave their clients on methadone indefinitely. On the other hand, drug substitution during alcohol withdrawal can be completed within a week.

A drug-withdrawal regime will have best chance of success when there is a clear agreement about the need to reduce the drug dose, and about the time-scale involved. In general, it is best to respect the client's views when negotiating a withdrawal strategy. If a patient is keen to stop using drugs very quickly, then this view should be supported, with the option of some adjustment if the experience turns out to be too stressful.

During detoxification it is important that encouragement and re-assurance are provided by the PHC worker, friends, and relatives. The need for some form of psychological support cannot be overemphasized.

The support of friends and relatives is essential.

Specialized interventions

Social supports and relationships

A person with a drug- or alcohol-related problem needs to have regular contact with other people, who can often help simply by listening and giving encouragement. One role of the PHC worker is to identify people who might be able to help in this way. They might be relatives or friends, former drug users, a priest, or volunteers.

Another valuable role for the PHC worker is to encourage better communication between clients and their families. One simple method of helping people to communicate is outlined below.

Helping communication

If a husband and wife are communicating badly, the PHC worker should concentrate on teaching them ways of improving their communication skills. First of all select an object, such as a piece of fruit or a stone. Explain that only the person holding the stone is allowed to talk. Give the stone to the husband, who should then talk for about one minute. His wife should then take the stone and summarize what her husband said. When a correct summary has been made, the wife should continue to talk, expressing her own views for about one minute. She then passes the stone back to her husband and he summarizes her statement. This whole cycle is then repeated.

This simple strategy can help to develop good communication skills involving active listening and summarizing.

Helping a family usually involves the following components:

- increasing ability to communicate in order to solve family problems more efficiently;
- increasing the amount of praise, and the frequency of positive comments, within the family;
- reducing the frequency of conversations about negative incidents in the past.

Developing confidence in ability to change

Most people with drug or alcohol problems have tried to change many times. After repeated failures they usually experience feelings of helplessness whenever they try to change, or even when they think about trying. The PHC worker should discuss these feelings and provide encouragement and hope by:

- pointing out that nearly every person suffering from drug problems actually tries to stop many times before finally succeeding;

– discussing any small (or large) successes in the past and pointing out that the same can be achieved again;
– as treatment progresses, keeping an eye open for small successes, praising these, and encouraging the patient to keep trying;
– when a relapse occurs, pointing out that this is bound to happen from time to time; preventing relapse is a skill that has to be learned.

Clarifying reasons for changing

Some patients know exactly why they need to reduce their drug use. If this is the case, then they should be reminded of their reasons regularly and vividly. The following strategy can help:

- Identify the two or three main reasons why the patient should stop or reduce his/her drug or alcohol use. For example:
  – to save his/her marriage,
  – to improve health and fitness,
  – to save money in order to take a family holiday.
- Now find an activity that your patient does regularly every day (e.g., drinks eight cups of tea throughout the day).
- Ask your patient to think about the reasons for stopping or reducing drug or alcohol use and to build up a positive image, e.g., of a good marriage, a healthy body, or a happy holiday.
- Now ask him or her to bring these images to mind every time he or she has a cup of tea; in this way, the patient is more likely to have these images in mind when faced with a tempting situation.

Alternatives to drug use

If a patient lives alone and has no job, no friends, no interests, and no hope, commitment to change will be low and relapse will be likely. The PHC worker should try to get the patient to take up one or more pleasurable activities that do not involve drugs. One possible strategy involves the four steps outlined below:

- devise a short list of possible activities;
- select one or two activities that are of interest to the patient and can be easily taken up;
- obtain the patient's commitment to become involved in these activities;
- take a keen interest in your patient's achievements.

Initially, tasks should be small, specific, and achievable, e.g., walk to the next village and back on Monday, Wednesday, and Friday (**not** simply, go walking).

Encourage the patient to take up a specific activity.

Preventing relapse

One of the tasks of assessment is to identify high-risk situations and mood states that have, in the past, resulted in relapse. For example:

- a family row;
- when the patient is in the company of a particular person;
- when the patient has a whole weekend ahead with nothing to do.

The PHC worker and the patient should together try to think of ways of coping with or avoiding these situations. List possible coping strategies and then select the most appropriate ones. For example:

Problem: What to do about my desire to use drugs when I have nothing to do at the weekends?

Solutions: 1. Always plan weekends as far ahead as Wednesday.
2. If the desire to use drugs starts to increase, then take a bus to go and see an uncle in the country.
3. Think of the reasons why I have given up drugs when I am doing a pleasurable task, such as digging the garden.
4. Go for a very long walk.

Selection: 3 and 4.

Crises and relapse situations are bound to occur during the follow-up period. One approach to crisis intervention is to build on a simple but systematic approach to problem-solving, such as the one outlined above. Crisis intervention is described in more detail below.

Follow-up and after-care

Most patients suffer a relapse fairly early. After the first six months, relapse becomes increasingly less likely but can still occur many years after treatment.

Certain factors are associated with relapse. These include poor social and psychological adjustment, as well as incomplete removal of the factors that initially precipitated the disorder (e.g., the same drug-using peer group, the same crippling pain for which the drug was initially prescribed, the same level of depression or anxiety). Crises often occur unexpectedly and no amount of preparation will give absolute assurance that crises will not occur. The answer is prompt and adequate crisis intervention.

The procedure for crisis intervention (or clinical problem-solving) involves three stages:

- clarification of the problem;
- search for a solution;
- decision-making.

Clarification of the problem

- Allow the patient to tell the entire story in his or her own words.
- Help the patient to express fully his or her feelings about the problem: the patient's awareness of these feelings will be a key factor in resolving the crisis.
- Ask specific questions regarding aspects of the problem that you do not understand, that are not clear, or that the patient may not have considered.
- Rephrase the problem as you understand it, and see if the patient agrees with your assessment; if not, repeat the entire process outlined above until you can rephrase the problem in a form that the patient accepts.
- If the problems are complex and overwhelming, identify one problem that can be considered initially.

Search for a solution

- Ask the patient to name all the possible ways of resolving the problem.
- Mention any alternatives that may have occurred to you, but not to the patient.

- Help the patient to establish which parts of the problem are most important, and which are least important.
- Assist the patient in deciding which parts of the problem should be addressed immediately, and which can be left until later.
- Help the patient to decide what further information must be obtained in order to resolve the problem.

Decision-making

- Help the patient to decide which features of the problem can be changed, and which features must be accepted (at least temporarily, if not permanently).
- Counsel the patient to make as few far-reaching decisions (such as seeking a divorce or quitting a job) as possible during the period of crisis.
- Help the patient to make any decisions that are immediately necessary.
- Avoid making any decisions on the patient's behalf, unless there is a life-threatening situation (e.g., the patient is delirious or suicidal).
- Invite the patient back to see you at a specific time, in the near future, in order to assess his or her progress.

Many drug-dependent persons find that they are in conflict with others within their immediate environment. The PHC worker has an important role to play in mediating between the patient and these other individuals. The procedure is as follows:

- Get both sides to express their concerns in their own words; facilitate full expression of the problem, and clarify its nature, by asking questions.
- Ask the drug or alcohol abuser to describe what he or she wants to happen; this might be approval to return home or to resume work.
- Ask the affected person (e.g., family member, work supervisor) to describe what he or she wants to happen, as regards the patient; this might be the patient's return home or resumption of work.
- Inquire whether an agreement can be negotiated between the parties. For example, would the abuser cease drug or alcohol use in return for being reinstated in his/her job, and would the work supervisor reinstate the person if drug or alcohol use were discontinued?
- If the matter can be negotiated up to this stage, it is important to agree on a contingency plan in the event of relapse (since relapses are common, especially in the early stages of recovery). For example, the patient may be suspended from work, or asked to leave work for one week with the first relapse, two weeks with the second relapse and so on.

The basic rules in negotiating a contract:

– draw up very clear and specific rules;
– ensure that a change for the better is rewarding to all parties;
– agree that one or two lapses do not make the agreement null and void.

Finally, it should be emphasized again that, apart from the primary health care worker, there are usually a number of other local people who can be involved in the care and after-care of the client. These include religious and traditional leaders, traditional healers, law enforcement agents, and recovered clients. Religious and traditional leaders are usually very highly regarded, particularly in developing countries. They are guardians of opinion and behaviour, and their potential contribution should not be underestimated. They know most families within the community, and they can be very useful in tracing clients who default.

In many developing countries, patients still consult traditional healers more often than they do orthodox health workers. Community-based health programmes for drug- and alcohol-dependent persons are therefore meaningless unless they take account of the important role of traditional healers.

Law enforcement officers are usually seen as agents of punishment. This idea needs to be changed, since the police can be very helpful in a variety of ways. Also, recovered drug-dependent persons can often play a vital role in the treatment of others in the community. Such an activity can not only help the recovered person to stay off drugs, but also give the new patients the confidence and hope that they too can recover completely.

The PHC worker should be ready and willing to refer patients to specialist services, if these are available. Such referrals should be prompt and appropriate, and the PHC worker must therefore know about the existing specialist social and medical resources. Before referring a patient, the PHC worker should carefully explain why, and to whom, he or she is being referred, and what to expect. Therapists should be open and honest. They should enjoy their patients' confidence, and assure them that they will continue to provide help and support.

Total abstinence is not always possible in the short term, and the PHC worker should appreciate the value of a reduction in drug and alcohol use. Furthermore, many patients will fail. They should be encouraged to try again. Relapses are very common and may occur many times before the patient finally achieves success. The therapist should not give up.

6. Strengthening links between the health sector and law enforcement personnel

In many countries, primary health care personnel are actively engaged in health promotion within their community, but this work often does not cover drug and alcohol problems. Even when there is a community action plan for the prevention of drug- and alcohol-related problems, the law enforcement agencies tend not to participate fully. This chapter explains why the cooperation of law enforcement agencies is needed and how it can be achieved.

Prevention: the role of the primary health care worker

In recent years, great progress has been made by specialist health care services, but these advances have had relatively little impact in the field of prevention, particularly at community level. Furthermore, in countries where resources are limited, specialist services can ill afford to reach whole communities.

PHC workers, on the other hand, usually work within a well-defined locality, which they know well. They are in close contact with the members of that community, including community leaders and key individuals working within the various sectors, such as education and social services.

For these reasons the PHC worker is ideally placed to play a central role in preventive and harm-reduction activities in the field of drug and alcohol abuse in the community.

As described in Chapter 3, the functions of the primary health care service with regard to drugs and alcohol can be considered within the framework of three levels of prevention:

- **Primary prevention** aims to avoid the appearance of new cases of drug and alcohol abuse, by reducing the consumption of drugs and alcohol through health promotion.

- **Secondary prevention** attempts to detect cases early and to treat them before serious complications cause disability.
- **Tertiary prevention** aims to avoid further disabilities, and to re-integrate into society individuals who have been harmed by severe drug and alcohol problems.

The PHC worker will be involved at each of these three levels.

Although primary health care workers should play a key role in prevention strategies, they will need help from the start. The only sensible approach is to create a community action team in collaboration with other sectors including, wherever possible, the law enforcement agencies.

Law enforcement agencies

In most countries, several law enforcement agencies are involved in the prevention and control of drug abuse including:

- the police force,
- the excise department,
- the customs department,
- the immigration authorities,
- the armed forces (in some countries),
- the judiciary, and
- the prison department.

The **police force** is usually the most visible and active in this field. Police departments are responsible for implementing the laws concerned with drug and alcohol production and consumption. They are also involved in dealing with drug- and alcohol-related crime, and in crime prevention.

The **excise department** is directly concerned with matters pertaining to alcohol and, sometimes, to other drugs. It has the power to change the level of taxation on alcoholic drinks. The amount of alcohol consumed by a community decreases as taxation, and therefore the price, increases. At the very least, there should be discussions about this sort of issue.

The **customs department** is mainly concerned with the import and export of drugs and alcohol. It should be remembered, however, that even in situations where a country is only a transit point in the movement of drugs from one country to another, a certain amount of "spillage" is inevitable leading to increased availability at the transit point.

Immigration authorities have the power not only to prevent persons suspected of drug trafficking from entering a country, but also to deport and extradite suspected persons. In work connected with the control of availability, the customs and immigration departments often work together.

The **armed forces** are sometimes called upon to work in conjunction with immigration and customs authorities. Furthermore, in some countries, drug control policies are the responsibility of the ministry of defence.

The **judiciary and prison departments** are clearly involved, and their role is similar in most countries. Sometimes, drug use is a large problem within prison populations.

There is another issue that deserves attention. Personnel employed by some of these agencies have frequent and easy access to drugs and alcohol. Furthermore, the nature of their duties, and their life-styles, can make them vulnerable to drug or alcohol abuse. Therefore, PHC workers should not only seek their support but also view them as potential target groups for prevention and treatment.

Negotiation and shared objectives

The main reason for emphasizing cooperation with law enforcement agencies is that these agencies and the health sector actually have shared objectives and yet they rarely work together. Cooperation is possible because shared objectives can be identified.

First of all, before considering methods of influencing, and gaining the cooperation of, law enforcement agencies, consider an approach that is almost certain to fail. Imagine that you put the following proposal to a senior police officer:

> *"Since the police deal with a large number of people suffering from drug and alcohol problems, shouldn't you train your staff to take on a social work and a counselling role?"*

The police officer's response to this will undoubtedly be defensive. He or she might say, for instance:

> *"I joined the police force to enforce the laws of the land and not to be a social worker. I would be a laughing stock if I made such a proposal."*

What would be a judge's response to the following suggestion?

> *"We believe that drug and alcohol dependence should be treated like diseases. Prison is not the answer. It doesn't cure diseases, and, since drug use is prevalent in our prisons, it will just make matters worse. Your use of custodial sentences is wrong."*

Again, this rather confrontational approach is likely to invite a confrontational response.

A more realistic and effective method of gaining the cooperation of law enforcement agencies and organizations involves the following key ideas:

- **Understand objectives.** In order to influence any organization, it helps to know what key objectives the organization is working towards. Are community policing strategies being developed? Is there a desire among the judiciary to reduce the prison population?
- **Identify the key people.** The process of change within an organization usually involves one or more influential people with enthusiasm for a particular objective, who champion the cause. Attempts to find such people should be a crucial task.
- **Entry points.** A knowledge of the current objectives of an organization will suggest a way in. Some doors are half-open, but others are closed and bolted. Often an entry point will depend upon social concern and attitudes. For example, driving under the influence of drugs or alcohol is now generally considered to be dangerous and wrong. Police departments will be more inclined today, than thirty years ago, to discuss cooperation in this area.
- **Expanding the agenda.** Once entry has been gained, and relationships developed, it is much easier to consider a broad range of proposals involving cooperation between health workers and law enforcement personnel. For example, it may then be relatively easy to develop a youth club, or a football team, for drug abusers and others, in collaboration with the police.

Examples of cooperation with law enforcement agencies

Needle and syringe exchange schemes. A number of services have been set up throughout the world to prevent the spread of AIDS, by providing users of intravenous drugs with clean needles and syringes. Such a service can only be effective if the police keep their distance. This has usually been achieved through discussions at the highest level in the police force.

Access to treatment. In some communities, the police have agreed not to arrest drug users after a first offence, provided that they attend a drug service for treatment. In others, drug users held in a police cell are seen by a doctor involved in the drug service in order to discuss the treatment possibilities. Setting up such collaborative ventures can satisfy the police, the client, and the drug treatment service.

Collecting data. Both the law enforcement agencies and the drug treatment services are keen to identify the extent of the problem, the number of cases, and any new trends. There are numerous examples of the police and health services working together to collect relevant information and data.

Crime prevention. Setting up a training course can lead to some interesting cooperative ventures as the people attending the courses plan drug- or alcohol-related projects. One such project was planned by a psychologist and a senior policeman. The entry points were community policing and crime prevention. A number of bars in the centre of a town were targeted, and the police made regular visits. In a friendly way, they reminded bar staff about the laws relating to young people, as well as those relating to selling drink to people who were already intoxicated. This high profile community policing had quite a dramatic impact on alcohol-related crimes, reducing the number of arrests by over 20%.

Drink and driving. It is relatively easy to get the cooperation of various groups to develop a drink-driving campaign. One such campaign brought together the police, the brewers, bar staff, social workers, health promotion specialists, the transport industry, and a number of other groups and individuals. The campaign had a very high profile, but the most significant effect was the building up of momentum to such an extent that the drink-driving campaign was followed by a much more comprehensive "DRINK-WISE" programme. The police were determined to play a part

WHO 91194

A drink-driving campaign may be a useful starting-point for collaboration with the police.

in the drink-driving campaign, but were then linked into the broader prevention and health promotion initiative.

Licensing authorities. One interesting and unusual example of collaboration between the health services, the social services, and a law enforcement agency involved a committee that had responsibility for issuing licences to sell alcohol. Close cooperation and discussion resulted in the committee agreeing to provide licences only on condition that the prospective licensee attended a course on alcohol-related problems. These courses are now well established and valued by both the licensing authority and the licensees.

Influencing the gatekeeper

In most activities that involve community action, there are people in authority who can facilitate or hinder a particular project. For instance, it may be impossible for the police to develop a course on drugs for schools without the assent of the regional director of education. He or she is the gatekeeper for this type of project. Collaboration on a project will certainly be helped if the gatekeepers can be identified and involved in some way. Sometimes the decision to halt a project is a result of lack of information about the project and about the people involved. If the gatekeeper can put a face to a name, then he or she is much more likely to say "Yes".

Gathering information

Information is essential for effective preventive work, but quite a lot can be achieved, particularly at the local level, with minimal effort.

Some of the essential information may be already known to the PHC workers. Some of it will be known to law enforcement agencies and to key persons within them. There is, therefore, a clear advantage in cooperation right from the early stages of planning community action. The assessment of a community is dealt with in Chapter 2, but the following is a brief checklist of information that could be useful:

● *Characteristics of the population:* numbers, composition, economic status, employment, literacy, etc. Much of this information is known by PHC workers and the police.
● *Assets and barriers:* the proximity of harbours, airports, tourist resorts, counselling/treatment/rehabilitation facilities, educational institutions, nongovernmental organizations (NGOs), etc. The law enforcement

agencies will be able to indicate where the main drug problems are to be found, which drugs tend to be abused, and how health care workers could gain access to this network. It is also helpful to the law enforcement agencies to have a description of health and social care services and organizations.

- *Drug and alcohol consumption patterns, high-risk groups, and ensuing harm:* pooling information from various groups, including law enforcement agencies, could provide a very useful assessment of the drug- and alcohol-related problems within the community. This will also lead to ideas for improving the validity of the data.
- *Referral systems:* a chart displaying the current referral systems might be a very useful method of spotting gaps and developing new systems (e.g., referral from law enforcement agencies to the health and social care systems).
- *Skills audit:* it is useful to draw up a list of all the people who are willing to help, together with their specific skills. A particular police officer might be very good at collecting information and cross-checking for accuracy. A magistrate might volunteer to write documents. Some people may have been trained in counselling skills.

Getting together to share and collect information is an excellent way of starting a dialogue that can lead to creative ways of developing links between the health sector and law enforcement personnel.

Planning and working together

Developing good relationships and setting up small-scale projects are the two most important tasks that must be achieved if a number of agencies

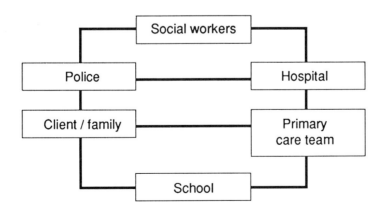

WHO 91195

A referral chart can be a useful method of identifying key people and spotting gaps.

are to work together. Only when collaboration is close and prolonged may it be helpful to plan other activities. These may fall under a number of headings, such as the following:

Assessment of needs. Is there a need for advice, counselling, or treatment? Are there gaps in the service or in education and training? Do the law enforcement agencies need a training course? It will not be possible to satisfy all of the identified needs, but this form of assessment will help the discussion of priorities.

Formulation of objectives. Objectives are formulated by combining the needs assessment with a knowledge of the resources and skills that can be provided by a community team. Whenever possible, the objective should focus upon an outcome as well as a process. For example:

- To plan and run a training course, *and* to train ten volunteer counsellors who will each be a key worker for one person with a drug or alcohol problem

NOT simply "to plan and run a training course".

Planning of action. Actions flow from objectives. They should be clear and concise and delegated to specific individuals. Ideally, actions should focus on short-term goals so that progress can be reviewed regularly. In a field as complex as drug abuse, action has to be taken on several fronts and, therefore, needs to be well coordinated. It is essential that one person takes responsibility for coordination.

Implementation. The main problems that have to be identified under this heading are resistance, lack of enthusiasm, and lack of cooperation. Also, problems are bound to arise that have not been anticipated. Regular telephone contacts and problem-solving meetings must be arranged.

Monitoring and evaluation. A very simple question needs to be asked when a programme of action is being planned: "How shall we know if we have achieved what we set out to achieve?" This is always easier to ask than to answer. Nevertheless, it is often possible to collect information from a number of sources that will answer this question.

Maintaining cooperation

Cooperation between agencies with different philosophies and roles can be very difficult. Collaboration is time-consuming and differences of opinion can lead to arguments, frustration, and even sabotage. It is, therefore, essential that strategies for maintaining cooperation are considered from the start; the following have been found to be useful in some settings and some countries.

- **Management support.** The probability of success is increased if there is collaboration at the highest levels and if the drug and alcohol projects are given high priority by senior managers. It also helps if both the health care workers and the law enforcement officers have to provide progress reports to senior managers within their respective organizations.
- **Focus on the benefits.** Many benefits ensue from collaboration, but it is easy to lose sight of them. It is essential that the members of a community action team are regularly and frequently reminded of these benefits. It should be emphasized that looking at the drug problem from different angles can lead to new ideas, new approaches, and better information. The action team should be reminded of any small successes that have already been achieved, as well as the objectives that they are working towards.
- **Public image.** The public image of law enforcement agencies will benefit if they are involved in prevention activities. Some police officers are very keen to be involved in crime prevention as well as control. Cooperation will be enhanced if these preventive activities are given appropriate publicity.
- **Achieving small successes.** Motivation is continuously renewed when small-scale goals are regularly achieved. Any programme of action should thus be divided into small goals, otherwise a group may be overwhelmed by the enormity of the task that it faces. For example, a small-scale project might be "to add one question about drug and alcohol use to the form that is completed after every arrest". This could also be divided into smaller steps.
- **Motivational workshops.** It sometimes helps to pause and ask: Where are we now? Where do we want to be? How can we get there? Inviting senior managers and other key people to a workshop where these questions are addressed could help to clarify objectives and increase motivation.
- **Publicity.** Cooperative projects are often newsworthy and can provide an excellent subject for articles about drug and alcohol problems, and about the type of community action that is required.
- **Liaison with other action groups.** There may be other action groups within the community that have achieved successful collaboration between health and law enforcement personnel. The focus of such collaboration might have been a community event, such as a festival, or a community issue, such as the location for a power plant. Identifying these groups, and their methods of working, might suggest better ways

of facilitating collaboration. Such a group might also be encouraged to develop an interest in drug issues.

Conclusion

There are very good reasons why the health sector should collaborate with law enforcement agencies. Such cooperation is good for both agencies and for the community. Nevertheless, working together can be very difficult since totally different approaches and objectives are often adopted. When assessing the possibility of collaboration with law enforcement agencies, it is useful to ask the following questions:

- Has the agency ever considered a community and preventive approach?
- Are such approaches being considered at the moment?
- Have the deliberations actually resulted in action?
- To what extent has action been initiated and maintained?

If an agency has never considered a preventive programme, the way in which an approach is made needs to be radically different from an approach to an agency that is already involved in an active programme.

7. Simple evaluation of efforts to reduce drug and alcohol problems

When individuals, groups, or organizations work together it is usually assumed that they will have a greater effect than they would have working separately. While this may be true, it is most important that the programmes are carefully planned on the basis of good information, and that they are periodically evaluated to see if they are having the effects that were intended. Such planning and evaluation efforts can be quite simple, or they can be complicated and time-consuming. But they are essential if communities are to find out if their good intentions and hard work are producing the desired results in terms of fewer problems related to alcohol and drugs. If they are not, changes should be made to achieve better results for the resources invested.

Because evaluation sometimes implies a judgement as to success or failure, some people may be reluctant to undertake such activities in case the results indicate failure. While this, of course, occasionally happens, what is far more likely is that the results will show that some changes are necessary to improve the programme. Remember that even the best programmes can be improved through the planning and evaluation process.

The purpose of this chapter is:

- to describe the process of setting goals and objectives, as a basic tool for programme planning and evaluation;
- to outline the potential benefits of evaluations of various types and at various levels; and
- to provide information about a range of specific evaluation methods that readers can adapt to their own situations.

Once the basic concepts and techniques of evaluation are understood and have been practised, they will become easier and appear less threatening, and will lead to improved efforts to reduce alcohol and other drug problems.

Gathering information as the basis for planning and evaluation

When a community resolves to take action against alcohol and drug problems, it invests resources in the hope that the programmes it establishes will be beneficial. All too often, however, it is assumed that good intentions and the utilization of resources are all that is required. To be effective, the programmes need to be based on good information about the nature and extent of alcohol and drug problems in the community.

Therefore, gathering good information is the first task to be undertaken. The gathering of information can be quite simple and informal, or it can be very extensive, requiring special research skills. No matter what resources are available to a community, at least some basic information is required before programmes can be planned. Readers should also consult Chapter 2, which provides guidance on the collection of data about alcohol- and drug-related problems.

Types of information to gather

Three kinds of information will be important:

- the nature of alcohol and drug use in the community,
- the specific kinds of problem caused by their use and the kind of people affected by them, and
- what powers and influences in the community can be brought to bear on these problems.

More specifically, the answers to the types of question listed below will be valuable in planning and evaluating preventive activities:

- Which drugs are used? How are they taken? What are the characteristics of the users? What are the chief reasons for use? What is the pattern and environment of use? Are there specific trends in use (such as a new drug)?

  The more that is known, the more specfic the programme objectives can be, and the easier it will be to target preventive activities at particular high-risk groups or those with high-risk behaviour.
- What community problems are caused by drugs? Are there: health problems, such as cirrhosis or respiratory ailments? behavioural problems, such as absenteeism from school or work? family problems, such as domestic violence? work problems, such as poor performance or injuries on the job? financial problems, such as wages being spent on drink or drugs? legal problems, such as arrest? In general, the more that is known about the specific kinds of problem the better.

  Such information will help define where, within the community, alcohol and drug problems have their greatest impact, and who might take an interest in reducing such problems. Also, such information will be valuable, later, for gauging the success of the preventive activities.

- Which organizations make important decisions that could affect the use of drugs and alcohol? Who are the key decision-makers? How are price and availability of the various drugs determined? Which laws are relevant, and how are they enforced? Which professional and voluntary workers are interested in alcohol and drug problems? Which other individuals or groups (such as the mass media) might be willing to take action? What other health or social problems (such as child nutrition or AIDS) are affected by alcohol and drug use, and what organizations are involved in tackling those problems?

Gathering information to answer questions such as those listed above will help you to plan your intervention programmes, and give you a basis against which to measure your successes. Without this basic understanding, it will be difficult to establish realistic goals and objectives for your efforts, and it will be almost impossible to develop priorities.

Methods of gathering information

Many different methods may be used for gathering such information, from the very simple to the very complex. Sometimes, much of the information already exists in one form or another, perhaps in various reports or in the minds of people who have been studying or observing these problems for some time. In some areas with ample resources, it is possible to gather very comprehensive information prior to starting a preventive programme. In other areas, simple, inexpensive methods may need to be used (see Chapter 2).

How to gather the information necessary for evaluation

Some of the problems posed by alcohol and drugs are urgent, and require urgent action. Sometimes, it may seem that there is not enough time to gather all the relevant information before planning an action programme. However, the following procedures will help to ensure that best use is made of existing information and may help to avoid major mistakes in the rush to do something.

- Identify issues that are already well known. Make a list of the major issues and policies that are thought to be relevant to community problems, especially if they have not been acted upon. An example might be that schoolchildren seem to have easy access to various drugs and that nobody appears to be doing anything about it.

- Identify key individuals who are knowledgeable. Interview them to learn what they believe are the major problems and what short-term and long-term approaches might be worth while. Compile a list of their ideas. Useful people to interview would be religious and civic leaders, police, school principals, doctors and hospital administrators, business executives, and others who have probably seen the effects of alcohol and drug use. These individuals may be able to suggest other people to talk to, and may later be enlisted to support the community-wide effort.

- Review existing documents. Sometimes reports have been prepared by academics and professionals, but are not widely available. They might include information on certain types of problem, such as hospital emergency admissions, school truancy, and public awareness and concern about various health and social problems. These documents may provide important information about the problems, and about the people with experience in assessing them and trying to do something about them.

- Use the information gathered in the above steps to prepare a preliminary report. Use this report to generate ideas from community leaders about how to address alcohol and drug problems. Sometimes, such a report will have the effect of making prevention a high priority for the community. This can lead to the development of an action plan, which can become the focus for both immediate and long-term efforts to reduce alcohol and drug problems. The report may also serve to generate wide support and increased resources for the implementation of the plan, especially if all sectors of the community have been involved in the discussions and feel they have a stake in the preventive programme.

Typical uses for the information

Information gathered as described above can be very useful in planning, implementing, and evaluating a preventive programme. For example, suppose that you learn that, although there is relatively little inhalant use in your community, there is increasing use among schoolchildren in a nearby community, and that inhalants are becoming more easily available in your area. Because teachers and parents may not be familiar with the substances being inhaled, the practice of inhaling, or the immediate health or behavioural consequences, they may not be aware that there is a problem, and therefore may not be able to intervene. Thus, a programme to inform teachers and parents about the substances, their sources, the inhaling practices, and the signs of inhalant use might be of high priority as a preventive measure.

Or, suppose that you learned that workers at a local factory were spending most of their wages on alcohol on pay-day. While the consequences of such spending would hurt the families of the workers, it would also have a negative impact on the factory, in the form of reduced output. Thus, the factory manager may be interested in working with members of the community to reduce the heavy drinking, and may contribute resources to the effort that would not have been available if the programme had been directed solely at the drinkers in their drinking environment.

So, information gathering can have a very practical benefit in determining which particular alcohol or drug problems are most serious, and which should have priority. It can also help in organizing various parts of the community, once people learn how the problems are having a negative effect on society. Further, the information provides a basis for comparison later, to see just how effective the various parts of the programme have been.

Setting goals and objectives

Anyone planning a programme to reduce drug and alcohol problems will find it valuable to establish goals and objectives. These will be very helpful in describing the basis for action, as well as in specifying which particular problems or behaviour the programme is designed to change. Without specific objectives, it is very difficult to evaluate programmes and to improve their effectiveness.

Goals and objectives are subject to a wide range of definitions. Goals, for the most part, represent the overall aim of the programme, e.g., to reduce alcohol- and drug-related problems. Objectives represent specific, measurable milestones in the implementation of the programme.

It is helpful to differentiate between four major types of objective:

- outcome,
- behavioural,
- educational, and
- administrative.

Types of objective

Ideally, each type of objective represents a link in a causal chain that leads to a desired programme outcome. For example, an outcome objective might be to decrease the number of days of absence from work due to heavy alcohol use. A behavioural objective could be to reduce the number of drinking occasions that lead to missed work days. An educational objective might be to teach people about the relationship between drinking and lost productivity, and an administrative objective could be to provide the resources necessary for educational classes (e.g., a teacher, a room, publicity, etc.).

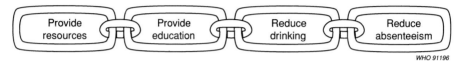

WHO 91196

The various types of objective are like links in a chain.

Clearly, these four objectives provide a range of opportunities for evaluation questions. Did the administration provide the necessary resources for the classes? Was the teacher effective? Why did only a few people show up? What kind of information did participants acquire? Did people like the class? Did they change their behaviour? Did the change in behaviour lead to a reduction in lost working days? These various ways of evaluating the activity will provide different measures of success. If few people attended the class, for whatever reason, it is unlikely that there will be any large-scale behaviour change, although those in attendance would be more likely to benefit. Likewise, if many people attended but the teacher was not well trained in delivering the necessary information, little behaviour change could be expected.

This chain of events is very important—the weakest link in the chain may undermine all the other efforts. Thus, evaluating the links in the chain can provide essential information about how to strengthen the weakest links, and therefore about how to contribute to reaching the overall goal. The value of evaluation, then, is to strengthen the overall programme to help it achieve its goals. Careful specification of objectives facilitates a good evaluation, and therefore provides the best chance of improving the programme over time.

Characteristics of objectives

While objectives can be of various types, they do have some features in common. They should be measurable, attainable, meaningful, appropriate, clear, and worth the effort. A clearly stated objective includes a specific time-period, a target population, and a desired effect. Agreement on programme objectives is an important first step in the development of a programme. Identification with the programme objectives is essential for workers to be able to understand the programme and to contribute meaningfully to its success.

Objectives should be:

measurable
attainable
meaningful
appropriate
clear
worth the effort

Types and levels of evaluation

Many types of programme evaluation are possible, and most good evaluation plans will combine several approaches in order to provide the most meaningful information. In many cases, each type of objective may require its own type of evaluation. Decisions will have to be made as to which efforts should be evaluated, as it will be impossible in most situations to evaluate all efforts because of lack of resources. A mix of the types of evaluation described below will be most beneficial.

Level 1: Activity. This most basic form of evaluation examines whether or not a programme is actually being carried out. Is there any activity to evaluate? Although this may seem odd, it is nevertheless relevant, especially in the case of new programmes. It often pays to check on activity, before moving on to the next levels.

Level 2: Inputs. This level of evaluation, and the next two levels, together assess programme operations. At this level, the resources being used to achieve the programme objectives are monitored. Resources might include funds, staff, facilities, equipment, services, materials, etc. Inputs should also include the number and characteristics of the programme participants. Too few or too many participants could lead to the ultimate failure of the programme, or at least to a review of the programme's objectives.

Level 3: Process. The process is often the main concern of the people who work with the programme on a daily basis, and the area in which most people have the greatest stake. Monitoring the programme process involves careful examination of the specific actions taken, by whom, for whom, with whom, how, when, and where. This level of monitoring may simply involve documentation, describing in detail exactly how people interact with the programme. This will make it possible to compare the way things are done with the way they were originally planned, in order to improve future programme efforts.

Level 4: Outputs. This level of evaluation is concerned with what comes out of the programme. Typically, this type of monitoring addresses such items as the number of people served by the programme, and the level and type of service received by different groups. It might also evaluate the more tangible products coming out of the programme, such as a curriculum, a television or radio message, or an employer's policy document.

Level 5: Outcome (or effectiveness). Much attention is usually given to this type of evaluation, which measures whether the programme has achieved the desired results. Has the programme had the intended effect on individuals, families, organizations, and communities? Has it reduced the actual problems, such as alcohol-related automobile crashes or inhalant use among schoolchildren? Many programmes generate very high expectations that they will reduce such problems, and there is disappointment if the evaluation does not show this. It may be unrealistic to expect every programme to reach such ideal goals, and it is also unrealistic to expect most evaluations to demonstrate that such goals were reached. Outcome evaluations are technically difficult and often require resources beyond the means of most community organizations.

Level 6: Impact. It is sometimes appropriate to look beyond the immediate scope of the programme to see if there have been any effects that were not planned or expected. An example might be the development of a company policy to provide free treatment for employees, after an educational programme for executives designed to reduce drunken driving among company employees. It is important to look also for negative consequences.

Level 7: Efficiency. No matter what has been achieved, or how it has been achieved, you may want to ask whether it was achieved as cheaply as possible. Was the maximum benefit derived from the resources invested? This is most useful when similar monitoring is applied to a range of programmes, in order to compare their efficiency. For example, what is the most efficient way to educate children about the harm that may result from drug use—through classroom activities or through after-school sessions? Cost per student may be one way to decide on the allocation of limited resources, if both ways are equally effective.

Effectiveness is doing the right things

Efficiency is doing things right

Thus, various types and levels of evaluation are possible for any particular programme objective. Some are relatively easy and quick; others are complex and require a lot of resources. The community action team will have to choose the methods that best suit their purposes, given their programme objectives.

For example, a programme to educate parents and teachers about inhalant use among children might not need to monitor programme impact or efficiency, because the main objectives would probably be to increase the parents' and the teachers' ability to recognize the substances and practices associated with inhalant use. The evaluations should concern the activity (Did the educational sessions actually take place?), the inputs (What resources were required?), the process (What actually happened during the educational sessions? Did they take place as planned? What unexpected needs were there? What can we learn from those sessions to improve any future sessions?), and the output (How many parents and teachers attended? What was their level of interest and concern? What educational materials were produced, in what quantities, and how can they be improved?).

Not all evaluation steps will be necessary, or fruitful, for each programme activity. The most important consideration is that the evaluation should be done carefully and with a clear purpose. In the above example, perhaps only one or two levels of monitoring are practical. In that case, process and output evaluation would perhaps be most beneficial, as they would suggest how well the programme was accepted (by counting the number of persons who attended, as the best single measure of interest on the part of parents and teachers).

Evaluation priorities

Just as each goal and each objective of a programme will be allocated a priority, evaluations should also be ranked. Thus, with limited resources, certain choices have to be made. Some evaluations may be useful, but not essential. Others may not be possible with the resources available. Others may be important, but there may be a lack of technical expertise to carry them out. The rule of thumb should be that, as with objectives, only those evaluations that are feasible and worth the effort should be undertaken.

Objectives for the health worker

One way to decide which evaluations should be carried out is to review what types of effect the key elements of the programme are having. For example, the primary health care worker—who is, perhaps, the main

83

resource of the programme should attempt to assess his or her role in the overall development of the programme. Specifically, it might be worth preparing personal objectives to assess achievements over a particular period. This will allow the individual to monitor his or her own progress in meeting realistic objectives.

For example, for some PHC workers a major objective will be to persuade community leaders from various sectors to become involved in the programme to reduce alcohol and drug problems. This might mean developing an intermediate objective to meet three leaders from health, police, religious, civic, educational, or nongovernmental organizations within the first three months, with a further objective of persuading at least two people from each sector to join the community action team. Or the intermediate objective might be for specific levels of new resources to be contributed to the community action team for its use.

Defining one's own contribution to the overall community programme in this way may be especially helpful in cases where overall progress is hard to achieve, and harder yet to measure. Because alcohol- and drug-related problems are often intractable, and improvements are sometimes difficult to see, the PHC worker should know that he or she is on the right track and is accomplishing specific tasks that will contribute to the long-term reduction of problems. The primary health care worker should not be discouraged if after a year's work there are still alcohol and drug problems in the community, or even if the problems seem to get larger. This may happen as people become aware of the problems in general, and the stigma and the denial are reduced. A preventive programme will sometimes lead many people to seek treatment, as they or their families recognize for the first time that they have a drinking or drug problem. In this case, monitoring of the problem may show that it is growing, whereas in fact it is merely becoming visible for the first time. The primary health care worker should, therefore, not become discouraged, but should develop some personal objectives for periodic assessment to show that progress is being made, no matter how things may look from other perspectives.

Objectives for the community

Another measure of success is the degree of involvement of different sectors within the community in helping to reduce the problems. Ideally, all sectors of the community will come to recognize the problems of alcohol and drug abuse and will want to contribute to programmes to reduce such problems. Thus, in an evaluation of the process, involvement of community organizations can be a very useful measure, even if apparent alcohol and drug problems are not yet being reduced.

A long-term commitment to solutions involving all sectors of society is essential. This commitment should cover the availability of things like staff, equipment, and facilities, as well as funds. While it may be very helpful to get a commitment of financial resources from a local business, it would be equally valuable to be assured of the dedication of a part-time staff member from another business who could help carry out some of the tasks necessary for a preventive programme, or the use of an office or meeting place.

Likewise, members of a local organization may be willing to contribute their time, but they should be trained and monitored to ensure that the quality of service they provide is good. Evaluation of such free services might appear ungrateful, and some people may not wish to be monitored in this way. Yet, if the job is important, it is important to do it correctly. Well-meaning individuals can sometimes harm a programme, despite their best intentions. For example, many people believe that "scare messages" delivered to school-age children, emphasizing the horrible effects of drug use, are effective in discouraging children from trying drugs. But careful research indicates that this is not the case. A well-meaning teacher who delivers scare messages to children is, at best, wasting time and energy, and, at worst, may increase the children's curiosity about drugs.

Outside the community

Communities can learn from one another, and can benefit from one another's successes and mistakes. One community may decide that its highest priority in a preventive programme is education of schoolchildren about the harm caused by use of a particular drug. However, even with a highly sophisticated evaluation, it may be difficult to determine whether the programme has had any effect in terms of diminished drug use (outcome evaluation). In this case, it would probably be more useful to evaluate the activity, the input, the process, or the outputs. Assuming that the programme managers were able to demonstrate the feasibility of such a programme, a neighbouring community might be encouraged by this success to adapt the programme for its own use. This is an unexpected outcome which should be included in an evaluation report.

Evaluation in action

An example is given below to illustrate objectives and evaluations for a typical preventive activity. The approaches described may be more complete than many community action teams would find possible in their particular circumstances. Some community action teams, however, may have far more comprehensive objectives and evaluations in their plans. Parts of the example given below may be relevant to the needs of particular communities, but it is once again emphasized that each community action team should devise its own objectives and evaluation activities to meet its own needs. A key point to remember is that all evaluation efforts should be designed to improve the activities evaluated.

An example of a preventive activity—the mobile education unit

In one developing country, a community action team found that, although many people in the community understood the health and social consequences of drug use, they did not recognize the typical behavioural signs and did not know about the treatment available. In addition, many people in the community were worried about school-age children being exposed to drugs and being pressured to use them. So the community action team decided that a mobile education unit would be a good way to educate the public and to help protect the children. A vehicle was prepared, equipped with posters, booklets, a short video, and a puppet show, to travel from school to school within the community, so that the children, their parents, and others in the community could learn more about drug problems, and how to prevent, recognize, and treat them. The team wished to evaluate how well the activity accomplished its objectives so that decisions could be made about how to improve it, or whether to allocate resources to another activity.

WHO 91197

One approach to prevention is the mobile education unit.

The community action team decided upon the following basic objectives, as priorities:

- *Outcome objective:* within two years, the number of children in the
  community using drugs will have been reduced by 20%.
  While everyone agreed that this was an important objective, no one
  knew what proportion of children were using drugs at the beginning of
  the programme, and it was clear that it would use most of the available
  resources to find out. It would also be expensive to conduct another
  survey two years later, and even then they would not be able to
  attribute any change to the proposed mobile education unit. So,
  although this objective was believed to be important, the CAT decided
  that it would not be practicable to try to evaluate it directly.
- *Behavioural objective:* within two years of the start of the programme,
  over 80% of the children who say that they experienced pressure to use
  drugs will have been able to resist it.
- *Educational objective:* within one year, 80% of children in community
  schools will be able to identify the major drugs used, know the negative
  effects of their use, recognize the signs of use, know where to get
  treatment, and know how they can resist pressure from peers or others
  to use drugs.
- *Administrative objective:* within three months, the materials and equipment for the mobile unit will be ready for use, the individuals who will
  conduct the educational sessions will have been trained and have
  conducted at least one pilot session, and a schedule for presentations at
  all schools in the community will have been developed.

Developing evaluation methods

There are several possible ways of evaluating whether each objective has
been met. An evaluation could address several objectives at once. For
example, if the children can be tested in the classroom, a questionnaire
could be developed to test their knowledge of the harmful effects of drug
use, what drugs are commonly used in the community, how they would
recognize use of drugs, and related items. Such questions would all relate
to the educational objective. The children could also be asked questions
about whether they had ever been offered drugs or pressured to use drugs,
and how they had resisted that pressure. This information would relate to
the behavioural objective.

For the administrative objective, a series of related "milestones" might
be identified, such as:

— informing the community at large about the mobile unit through the
  media (in order to attract a wide audience),

Children's knowledge can be tested in the classroom.

— ensuring that all those who will present the programme are given training,
— preparing adequate quantities of materials to hand out to participants.

Similar milestones should be identified for each of the evaluation activities, to ensure that all the tasks are on schedule. For example, a questionnaire for use in the classroom will have to be prepared, tested, and duplicated, and teachers will have to be told how it should be distributed and completed. Someone must be assigned the responsibility for collecting and analysing the questionnaires, and for preparing a report.

These objectives and their evaluation might have been described differently, and other objectives might have been developed. For example, different targets might have been set for different age groups, or the evaluation might have considered only children in a specific age group, even though the educational activity would be available to all children. The CAT might have developed an educational objective for parents and other adults in the community. However, the results might have been difficult to evaluate. Another type of activity, such as special educational sessions in work or religious settings, would probably be more beneficial for parents. This is a good example of setting priorities for both the preventive activity and for the related evaluation. Priorities should be determined when objectives are set, and evaluations should be designed to determine how well the activity accomplished its particular objectives.

Limitations of the evaluation

In the above example, certain conclusions can be drawn at the end of the activity. Each of the objectives will or will not have been met, according to specific evaluation criteria. Assuming for the moment that all of the objectives were achieved, does that answer all of the questions the community action team might have about the success of the activity? With limited resources, the team probably could not cover all of the objectives, and also was not able to include all of the evaluations that it might have wished.

Assuming that the community action team was pleased with the success of the activity, it still might wish to know the answers to the following questions:

- Did we set the targets high enough? Should we be satisfied with just 80%? Will that level be maintained in three months or six months? How could the mobile unit have been more effective? Would the use of colour posters or more puppets in the show have made a difference?
- Could we have used our resources more effectively for other activities? Might it have been better to hold the sessions indoors, for example in a religious setting, where the children would have been more under control? Should we have developed a local radio programme instead? Or should we have provided resources to the police, so that they could have tried to reduce the availability of drugs to school-age children?
- Did the questionnaire accurately report the resistance of the children to pressure? Did the activity really have any effect in reducing drug use? What about those children who have already dropped out of school—aren't they even more likely to be using drugs?

These questions, and many more, may occur to the community action team. But with limited resources, there is only so much that can be done to develop and evaluate an activity. This is why it may be most useful to concentrate on evaluation of input, process, and output—essentially, on documentation of programme operations, on what resources went into the activity, and on how the products and services were used. Outcome evaluation is of course desirable, but all too often is impossible to achieve with limited resources.

Using the results of evaluation

Evaluation is intended to improve the preventive activities and pro-grammes. In the example above, the results of the various evaluations can be used to arrive at decisions to modify the activity so that it becomes more effective, or to put the resources into another activity instead. Such decisions involve judgements about the worth of activities and how best to reach the overall goal to reduce alcohol and drug problems.

For example, we might learn from the results of the evaluations that 80% of the schoolchildren did indeed learn about the major drugs, the harm they cause, the signs of use, and the benefits of treatment. Suppose, however, that relatively few children were able to say specifically how they would resist pressure from schoolmates or others to use drugs. This might be viewed as a major shortcoming, since a positive attitude in this respect is important to the success of the programme.

The community action team, on reviewing this information, might become discouraged and decide to cancel the project, or they might increase their efforts to strengthen the confidence-building part. They might decide to ask selected student leaders to demonstrate how to resist pressure to use drugs. A script could be prepared. Teachers and parents could be enlisted to work with children to build refusal skills. A radio programme popular with children might be encouraged to review the arguments against using drugs. Such efforts could expand an already worthwhile activity into a much more valuable programme, which could eventually contribute meaningfully to the behavioural objectives, and perhaps even the outcome objectives. The main point here is that the results of the evaluation should help decision-making on how to strengthen the activity.

The evaluation results could also be used in making judgements about which activities should be continued in future years. Using the above example, we might say that the cost of reaching each child in the community was x dollars. Could these resources be used more wisely in some other activity? What about a radio programme, or training parents to talk to their children about drugs, or setting up a recreational centre to provide alternative activities for children? The evaluation of the mobile unit will provide useful information about that activity, but of course cannot provide information about other activities that have not been tried.

It should be emphasized that evaluations are designed to provide objective information that the community action team can use to make important judgements. In addition, evaluation results can be used to advocate certain activities or programmes, by showing their success in achieving objectives. The organizations that supply funds for preventive activities like to be sure that their donations are helping to reduce alcohol and drug problems in the community, if only through the accomplishment of certain process objectives. Thus, a description of what actually took place—number of persons reached, number of booklets and posters distributed, changes in awareness and knowledge levels—can be used in seeking additional resources to continue or improve an activity, or to design a new programme based on what was learned. Evaluation results of this type should not be overlooked, because they can demonstrate quite powerfully that the activity is worth doing and is contributing to the accomplishment of the larger goals of the programme.

Summary

Evaluation of community preventive activities is not easy, but with adequate initial planning and objective-setting can be a valuable, realistic task. It can be argued that any preventive activity that is worth doing is worth doing well, and that the additional efforts made at the outset will be well rewarded later on, as the community action team will be able to see meaningful results of their efforts.

Specific objectives can be set for individual members of the community action team, for the team as a whole, for the community, and beyond. The benefits of setting such objectives will be to ensure that the preventive activities are wisely planned, well understood, realistic, and measurable. Further, they will help the community action team keep on track, will allow periodic review, with the opportunity to reset the objectives within certain limits, and will help to maintain enthusiasm when the overall prevalence of alcohol and drug problems may seem to be increasing no matter what is done.

8. Training primary health care workers to deal with drug and alcohol problems

While this manual is aimed mainly at primary health care workers, it can also be used to train other health workers, including nurses, midwives, health educators and health visitors, pharmacists, medical social workers, counsellors, and physicians. The manual can be distributed as a self-contained work of reference or it can be elaborated to meet the training needs of particular groups; however, it will be most effective if it is used as the basis for a training course. Trainers should modify the manual to cover substances in local use, and the local problems that are associated with excessive use of drugs or alcohol.

Whether they are providing in-service training or more formal education, trainers should be familiar with a variety of teaching methods and be able to function effectively in the lecture hall, small group discussions, and in a supervised, skills training situation. Role-modelling is particularly important in this kind of training.

Alcohol and drugs are psychoactive substances that can cause severe personal and social problems, and are often used together. In many areas where drug abuse has been traditional, alcohol abuse is now appearing. At the same time, drug use has increasingly accompanied alcohol use in areas where drinking has been customary. In some cultures, alcohol is a prohibited drug; in other cultures, alcohol consumption is socially accepted while other forms of drug use are not. In developing a training curriculum or adapting this manual, information specific to the local situation should be added and irrelevant information omitted.

Training primary health care workers to deal with drug problems involves not only imparting information and skills, but also developing an interest in the problems, as well as confidence in their ability to cope. Both confidence and interest grow slowly through positive experiences. This final chapter provides advice on the creation of such learning experiences.

Trainees should be viewed as participants rather than as students. The approach that will be outlined involves active participation in problem-solving exercises, role-playing, negotiations, assessment, and therapy, as well as a practical project designed to develop knowledge, skills, and confidence. Usually, the facilitator and the participants will be learning together.

It is assumed that other chapters of this manual will be used to prepare students for a training event. This chapter describes a range of exercises that could be used to consolidate and build upon the information provided in the earlier chapters. Some of the exercises involve three individuals—two actors and one observer who comments on the interaction. The observer's task is mainly to identify and describe successes so that everybody learns from them. Critical comments should be kept to a minimum, and should be given in the form of suggestions for improvement. A few of the exercises could be developed into projects.

Developing a curriculum

The aims and objectives of a training course must be tailored to the needs of the particular community, and to the level of knowledge and skills of the participants. A curriculum for primary health care workers should cover four broad areas:

- assessment of the problem in the community,
- assessment and counselling of the drug user,
- initiation and management of change at the community level, and
- evaluation of change.

For each of these areas, the objectives of a training course might be as described below.

Assessment of the problem in the community

The course should enable the primary health care worker:

- to be familiar with the drugs being used in the community, the ways they are used, and the attitudes in the community towards their use and abuse;
- to identify groups at risk of developing drug problems (e.g., young people, the unemployed);
- to identify other factors influencing drug use and abuse (e.g., social pressures, price, and availability).

Assessment and counselling of the drug user

The course should aim to:

93

- develop the skills required for effective communication with those who are abusing alcohol or drugs, in order to increase their motivation to change;
- develop the skills required for the primary health care worker to be able to communicate effectively with, and offer support to, the families of such persons;
- provide information about referral of abusers of certain drugs for detoxification, if the appropriate service exists;
- enable the primary health care worker to provide continuing care, in order to prevent relapse, and to deal with recurring problems;
- enable the primary health care worker to identify drug and alcohol problems at an early stage, and make early interventions.

Initiation and management of change at the community level

The course should also cover ways of:

- identifying resources in the community that could be used or mobilized to reduce drug- and alcohol-related problems;
- increasing awareness of drug- and alcohol-related problems in the community (e.g., through health education);
- identifying specific occasions and situations that lead to the early or habitual use of alcohol and other drugs;
- generating community action to reduce the influence of such occasions and situations;
- generating other community activities and social changes designed to reduce or prevent drug- and alcohol-related problems.

Evaluation of change

The course should train the students in:

- gathering evidence and information to help set objectives;
- setting targets and objectives;
- appreciating the limitations of evaluation;
- using the results of evaluation.

All of these elements of a curriculum for primary health care workers have been covered in the other chapters of this manual. The earlier chapters provide the background material and guidance. This chapter provides some examples of exercises that should help to develop knowledge and skills within the four areas outlined above.

Assessment of the problem in the community

Exercise 1: Key people and groups

For this exercise, it is assumed that one or two people know a particular community very well. A small group should play the part of a community action team that is listing all the key people and groups who could help to assess the drug and alcohol problems in the community; these key people might be a particular teacher, a doctor, a police officer, and a journalist with an interest in these problems. Is there a parents' group, or an Alcoholics Anonymous group, that might be interested?

When the key people and groups have been identified, the next task is to devise an interview checklist, or schedule, that could be used when asking for advice and information.

Exercise 2: A directory of services and resources

Many service providers are willing and able to help drug abusers, but primary health care workers often do not have the relevant information to hand. A project to produce a small booklet describing these services would help to clarify the needs of drug abusers, and how these needs could be matched with existing services. The first task would be to draw up a checklist of needs, such as the following:

- counselling
- marriage guidance
- befriending, or social support
- casualty and emergency services
- a self-help group
- leisure activities
- financial advice

This exercise might lead into a longer-term project, with two people collecting the relevant information.

Exercise 3: Assessing attitudes

The attitude of the participants towards drug and alcohol abusers might be considered. The following exercise may be useful in exploring misconceptions and in encouraging appropriate attitudes. It will also help in understanding the negative attitudes of a community towards drug abusers.

Ask participants to say the first three words that come into their mind upon hearing the following:

- drug,
- intoxicated,

- overdose,
- addict,
- alcoholic.

Ask the participants to rate a diabetic patient, a surgery patient, and a drug- or alcohol-dependent patient as follows:

	Strongly disagree	Disagree	Neutral	Agree	Strongly agree
Strong					
Compliant					
Friendly					
Honest					
Appreciative					

Ask the participants to describe three drugs and patterns of use that are acceptable in their communities, and three drugs or drug-use patterns that exist but are socially unacceptable.

Show examples of local advertisements for socially acceptable drugs. Note how they appeal to the reader's prestige, sexuality, or self-image.

The aim of this exercise is to identify misconceptions and to promote sympathetic understanding. By emphasizing the similarities between drug abuse and other common activities, such as the use of tobacco, or even over-eating, participants will be able to link drug abuse to their own personal experience.

Assessment and counselling of the drug user

The main point of these exercises is to develop the skills involved in identifying and helping people who are just starting to have drug or alcohol problems. If help for drug problems can be provided before the habit really takes hold, then the person can often be guided away from drugs and many years of suffering will be prevented.

Exercise 4: Identifying and assessing the drug problem

One participant plays the role of a drug abuser who is, perhaps, drinking alcohol every day and using cocaine at weekends. This participant should build up a clear picture of the problems caused by drug use, as well as the high-risk situations that lead to excessive use. The drug user should resist revealing everything all at once.

A second participant takes on the role of a nurse who is asking questions about general health, nutrition, social activities, and relationships. This person should help the drug user to identify threats to his or her health, as well as opportunities for change to a healthier life-style. The nurse should be warm and interested, but should, at the same time, act like a detective and follow up any relevant clues. For example:

Drug user: *"I'm not really aggressive, but I did get into a fight about two weeks ago."*
Nurse: *"What day of the week was this?"*
Drug user: *"Saturday about midnight."*
Nurse: *"Could you tell me what led up to this incident?"*
Drug user: *"Well, we started drinking on Saturday at lunchtime, and then at about 10 o'clock we went on to Tom's house . . ."* etc.

The nurse should attempt to get a clear picture of the extent of drug use, the problems associated with it, and the high-risk situations that are associated with excessive use.

The observer should make a note of questioning that leads on to revelations about drug use, and should identify questions or comments that put the drug abuser on the defensive.

The aim of this exercise is to ask questions slowly and gently about drugs, in the context of an interview about general health.

Exercise 5: Motivational interviewing

This exercise follows on from Exercise 4.

The aim of this role-play is to learn how to encourage drug or alcohol abusers to want to change, while, at the same time, avoiding confrontation. The first part of this exercise demonstrates what happens when a client is confronted.

(a) Two people are briefed separately. The first is told that she (or he) has a drug problem, but is not sure that she wants to change and is not sure that she would be able to change even if she wanted to. The second is told to try to get the drug abuser to change by giving a short, sharp warning about the horrific consequences of drug abuse. This interviewer should attempt to get over the message that total abstinence is the only real choice. For example:

"You are an addict, there is no doubt about that. I want you to stop using drugs today. Let me tell you what the consequences will be if you don't."

The therapist should keep up this confrontational approach and the observer should keep a note of the addict's response.

(b) The second part of the exercise involves a different approach which is sometimes called "motivational interviewing", since the aim is to motivate the individual to change gradually. This time the therapist guides the drug user by asking questions about physical, psychological, and social problems, and links these to drug use. For example:

Therapist: *"A few months ago you said that you had a major argument at least once a week with your husband. Now, you've just said that your husband cannot tolerate your drug use. Do you think that there is any link between the problems in your marriage and your drug use?"*

Drug user: *"Could be."*

Therapist: *"In what way do you think they are linked?"*

LONG PAUSE

Drug user: *"My husband says that our marriage was OK until I met Mary and started to use drugs."*

Therapist: *"To what extent would you agree?"*

LONG PAUSE

Drug user: *"I know that we will be divorced within a year if things go on as they are, but if I don't use drugs I'll be so irritable that we would split within weeks."*

Therapist: *"Well let's talk about how to reduce your irritability; and also I want to ask if your husband would be willing to see me."*

The aim of this exercise is to practise the skill of helping a drug abuser to link present and future problems with drug use, to consider reasons for changing and possibly to make a commitment to change. The first part of the exercise should demonstrate how confrontation can encourage a drug abuser to rehearse reasons why he or she should not, or cannot, change.

Exercise 6: Simple coping skills

The aim of this exercise is to use a systematic problem-solving approach to identify ways of coping with high-risk situations or moods that result in excessive drug use.

(a) Identify high-risk situations

The group should discuss the kinds of situation that lead to excessive use, and identify two specific ones, such as the following:

- It is lunchtime on a Saturday. You are bored and lonely. You know that you could visit your drug-using friends and feel very tempted.
- You have a row with your wife and feel like walking out of the house and visiting Sam. You know that Sam will offer you cocaine.

(b) List a variety of ways of dealing with these tempting situations. For example:

- Always plan your weekend on Thursday. Make sure that you will be involved in a variety of activities, and have something to look forward to.
- Start a hobby, get enthusiastic about some activity, or join a group (e.g., walking, swimming, local history).
- Ask the local priest, or a friend, if you could telephone him or her for a brief chat when you are tempted to use drugs.

(c) Discuss which activities or solutions stand the best chance of being successful.
(d) Mentally practise these solutions. For the drug abuser, repeated practice ensures that the coping skill is ready when needed.

This approach to developing coping skills can be used with individuals or groups. It can be carried out in just a few minutes, or could be the basis for a more extended discussion of high-risk situations and coping strategies.

Exercise 7: Communication skills

This is a very simple exercise which ensures that two people listen to each other, understand each other, and that each allows time for the other to present an argument or a point of view. The role-play involves a husband and wife who usually do not listen to each other, and do not communicate well. The wife is given an object (e.g., a stone or a piece of fruit). Only the person holding the stone is allowed to talk. The wife should talk for approximately one minute and explain, for example, why she gets annoyed when her husband is two hours late home and doesn't let her know in advance. The husband then takes the stone and briefly summarizes what his wife has said. If the summary is not accurate, it should be corrected by the wife. When a correct summary has been made, the husband then continues for one minute expressing his views. The whole cycle is then repeated.

This simple strategy can help to develop better communication skills, involving active listening, summarizing, and not interrupting.

Role-play can be a useful way of improving communication skills.

Initiation and management of change at the community level

In addition to the information provided in Chapter 4, the following exercises might be useful in learning how to mobilize the community.

Exercise 8: Identifying activities

Assume that one or two people have detailed knowledge of the particular community that is being considered. Following on from Exercises 1 and 2, which focused on key people and resources, the aim of this exercise is to propose a number of small-scale changes that could be implemented by a community action team. The emphasis must be on specific, achievable, small-scale proposals. For example:

● Commission an article on the relative strengths of the alcoholic drinks that are commonly sold in the particular community or country. Include information on sensible drinking.

100

- Find a doctor (e.g., in a casualty service) who might be interested in setting up a simple project to identify people with drug or alcohol problems.

The list that is produced might be long and overwhelming. The next stage of this exercise is, therefore, to select those activities that would lead to the greatest benefits, using an acceptable level of resources (e.g., time and money).

Exercise 9: Negotiating skills

An important task for a community action team is to negotiate with key individuals and groups. The basis of successful negotiation is the exploration of common objectives; for example, a simple exercise would be to ask the participants to imagine that the community action team is negotiating with a number of groups or organizations (e.g., those who sell alcohol, parents, employees, drug users, the police). Take each group in turn and work out common objectives; for example, both the community action team and the parents want children to say 'No' to drugs. Both want no violence or crime within the community. This task could easily lead to a number of role-play exercises; one participant could play the role of a journalist while another tries to persuade him or her to join the community action team. The team member should focus on common objectives, i.e., those that help the team and help the journalist. What does the journalist want? What would be a good story? What would be well received by members of the community? Would they be interested in a series of articles on drug problems?

Evaluation of change

Chapter 7 of this manual focuses on the evaluation of change. Since this is an important area that is usually feared and avoided, each participant could be responsible for a small project to monitor changes.

Exercise 10: Monitoring a day's training

Before the start of a day of training, an attempt could be made to develop a way of describing and assessing the day's activities:

What is the input?

How much preparation was involved?
How many hours were participants away from work?
Did it cost anything to hire a room?
What materials were specially prepared?

How can the process be described?

What information was imparted?
Which exercises were used?
How did participants interact?

What were the outputs and outcomes?

Which exercises were thought to be most useful?
At the end of the day, was there an increase in confidence and intention
to be involved in drug services?
What new ideas were produced?

Sufficient information should be collected to write a report on the day,
and to provide guidance on modifications that would be required if the
training were to be repeated.

Monitoring skills could also be practised by encouraging participants to
offer a supervised monitoring service to a local team or individual.
Alternatively, one participant might evaluate a project carried out by a
fellow student.

Another exercise could be to identify people within, for example, a
college, a university, or a factory, who have developed monitoring skills
and would be happy to supervise a participant.

Following on from the course

A course can be stimulating and informative and yet produce no
noticeable changes in the attitudes or behaviour of the participants. If
their colleagues are not supportive, and if the system is working against
them, it is easy to lapse back into old and comfortable habits. Fortunately,
there are a number of ways in which changes can be consolidated.

First, if possible, it is useful to train together two or three people from
one locality or service. Again, whenever possible, a manager and a trainer
should be included. In this way a small group of people can support each
other, and managers will be aware of changes that are being made to their
service or organization.

Secondly, participants should keep in touch after the end of the course.
They might even produce a newsletter to keep each other informed.

Thirdly, wherever possible, participants should get involved in successful local services. Enthusiasm will be increased by seeing examples of good
practice and meeting individual drug abusers who are recovering. It
might be very helpful to speak to the family of a recovering drug user, in
order to get a picture of family life before and after drug involvement.

A training course should be not simply a way of imparting knowledge, but also the first step in changing a service or a community.

Commonly abused substances

The classes or groups of psychoactive substances that can be abused and cause problems are diverse. The main classes and general characteristics of the various substances are described below.

Depressant substances

This group includes alcohol, barbiturates, and an enormous variety of synthetic sedatives and sleeping tablets (hypnotics). These substances have in common the ability to cause a degree of drowsiness and sedation, or pleasant relaxation, but may also produce "disinhibition" and loss of learned behavioural control as a result of their depressant effect on higher centres of the brain, a property that accounts for the apparent "stimulant" effects of alcohol. These drugs all have the potential to induce changes in the nervous system that lead to withdrawal symptoms, and the possible seriousness of these withdrawal states needs to be emphasized. Withdrawal from severe physical dependence on alcohol or barbiturates can be life-threatening.

Alcoholic beverages are widely used in many societies and because of this their abuse potential is often underestimated. Alcohol is a drug and must be used with caution.

"Minor tranquillizers" of the benzodiazepine type, such as diazepam or chlordiazepoxide, are probably best placed in the general depressant group, although they also have some distinctive features; the benzodiazepines have less potential to induce serious withdrawal states and are generally far safer in clinical practice than the barbiturates, although their dependence potential should be borne in mind.

Opiates (or opioids)

The prototype drug for this group is morphine, the major active ingredient in opium. Opium is the resinous exudate of the capsule of the white poppy, and contains, as well as morphine, other psychoactive substances that can be extracted in pure form, including codeine, a commonly used drug for relieving pain and cough.

Morphine can be converted, by a relatively simple chemical process, to heroin. Besides these opium derivatives, there are many entirely synthetic opiates, such as methadone (a drug used widely in the management of heroin abuse), pethidine (meperidine), and dipipanone. All the opiates have a capacity to relieve pain, produce a pleasant, detached, dreamy euphoria, and induce dependence. Withdrawal from opiates can be very distressing, but will not be fatal unless the patient is otherwise severely ill or debilitated.

Stimulants

Cocaine is the psychoactive ingredient of the coca leaf. It produces a sense of exhilaration and decreases fatigue and hunger. Similar effects are produced by a number of synthetic substances, such as the amfetamines and related substances, including phenmetrazine, methylphenidate, and various drugs that have been marketed for the treatment of obesity.

Khat is a shrub, the leaves of which are chewed in the Eastern Mediterranean region and East Africa. The active ingredient is cathinone, which has actions that are similar to those of amfetamine.

Cocaine, the amfetamines, and some of the synthetics can cause extreme excitement and induce short-term psychotic disorders. These substances have a high potential for dependence although the withdrawal symptoms seem to be limited to temporary feelings of fatigue, "let down", and depression.

Millions of people all over the world consume coffee and tea containing caffeine (tea also contains some theobromine). These substances tend to be stimulants, in that they alleviate mild degrees of fatigue, but they have a mechanism of action in the body that is quite distinct from that of cocaine and the amfetamines. Generally, they produce very low levels of dependence. Withdrawal symptoms, if any, seem limited to headache and fatigue.

Hallucinogenic drugs

This group includes LSD (lysergic acid diethylamide), mescaline, peyote, and certain other plant-derived or synthetic substances. These substances induce highly complex psychological effects, including transcendental experiences of "other-worldliness", hallucinations, and other types of perceptual distortions. Sometimes this experience becomes bizarre and frightening, producing what is commonly known as a "bad trip". These drugs do not induce physical dependence.

Cannabis

Cannabis is the generic name given to the drug-containing plant products of Indian hemp: this plant material contains an extraordinary array of psychoactive chemicals, the most important of which is tetrahydrocannabinol, or THC. The dried leaves or flowering tops are often referred to as marijuana or ganja, and the resin of the plant is referred to as hashish or "hash". Bhang is a drink made from cannabis. Cannabis appears to have some depressant qualities, but it can also have hallucinogenic effects. Until recently, it was believed that cannabis did not produce dependence but recent evidence throws some doubt on this belief.

Nicotine

Nicotine is another drug that merits a separate category. Nicotine can have a calming or sedative effect, but can also act as a stimulant. Nicotine readily induces a degree of dependence, but withdrawal symptoms are usually restlessness and irritability, rather than acute physiological disturbances.

Volatile inhalants

The volatile inhalants include anaesthetic gases, and the solvents in glues, lacquers, paint thinners, and so on. There is some doubt as to where to place these substances. They may have some depressant and anaesthetic effects, but they also seem capable of producing perceptual disturbances. Solvent sniffing can become a frequently indulged habit, but it is unclear whether any severe degree of physiological or psychological dependence develops. It is, however, a very dangerous habit because of the physical toxicity of the solvents.

Miscellaneous intoxicants

There are a few other drugs that do not fit neatly into any of the drug categories mentioned. Included here are kava, a substance used in some islands of the Pacific, and betel nut, which contains the drug arecoline and is widely used in Asia and the Pacific basin. Still another is the synthetic drug phencyclidine, currently popular among some groups of young people in the USA; in comparatively low doses it causes a mixture of drunkenness and anaesthesia, but in higher doses it causes psychotic states that may resemble schizophrenia.

ANNEX 2

Planning a survey

It has been pointed out that a community survey is a time-consuming and expensive business. It usually involves the following steps:

hiring support staff—developing and pre-testing the assessment schedule—training interviewers—pilot-testing—designing the survey and identifying the sample—data-gathering—checking and validation—data analysis—report-writing—dissemination.

The format of the questionnaire will depend upon whether the survey will involve interviews or self-administered questionnaires. The content of the questionnaire will depend upon the purpose of the exercise, but listed below are a series of information sets that you might consider collecting.

1. Demographic data

Age. Sex. Date and place of birth. Household composition. Marital status and family structure. Language(s). Ethnic or tribal status. Educational status. Religion. Employment. Previous encounters with police/courts. Residential circumstances and length of time at present residence. Health status.

2. Patterns of substance abuse

(The emphasis will be on obtaining details relating to recent substance abuse.)

● *Frequency/quantity*
Quantity. Seasonal or other fluctuation. Substances consumed. Frequency of abuse. Context of abuse (where? with whom?). Amount spent on these substances.

- *Consequences*
  Acute effects. Dependence. Reaction of others (e.g., medical, legal, familial). Effects on health. Injuries. Diseases.
  Consequences experienced as a result of someone else's involvement in substance abuse.

3. Attitudes towards substance abuse

- *Personal*
  Perceived good effects. Perceived harmful effects. Whether own abuse perceived as a problem. Sources of help perceived as available/useful.
- *Societal*
  Range of tolerance/ambivalence, qualified in terms of status of abusers (e.g., age, sex), situational context, occasion.

4. Social environment and personality variables

- *Social environment*
  Pattern of daily life, including leisure activities, aspirations with regard to work, housing, education, network of social contacts, political involvement.
- *Personality variables*
  Abbreviated measures of: self-esteem, sense of personal control, anxiety, depression, anger.

Community participation checklist

The following checklist can be consulted when a specific intervention is being planned. An ideal programme involves the active participation of the community at all stages. It should be developed by the community and not imposed upon it.

1. **Planning:** Is the programme being developed after the drug problem has been discussed with community representatives?
2. **Priorities:** Will the priorities be determined by the people themselves or by a government agency?
3. **Skills training:** Will training involve short local courses followed by regular in-service training or support? Alternatively, will the training be provided by a remote institution with no follow-up support?
4. **Implementation:** Will the programme be implemented with adequate community involvement?
5. **Monitoring:** Will the CAT be closely involved in the monitoring process?
6. **Ownership:** Is the programme perceived as a local programme developed by and for the locality?
7. **Representativeness:** Does the programme fully involve women, young people, the old, and the disabled?
8. **Communication:** Does an infrastructure exist for the exchange of information at the local level?